LIGHTS
in the
DARKNESS

— ⌘ —

LIGHTS
in the
DARKNESS

*For Survivors and Healers
of Sexual Abuse*

—— ℭ ——

SISTER AVE CLARK, O.P.

Resurrection Press
Mineola • New York

"Twelve Spiritual Steps" reprinted with permission from Dr. Joel Brande, M.D., Trauma Recovery Publications, Columbus, GA 31907.

The poem "Disciple of Jesus" is taken from *I Hear a Seed Growing* by Edwina Gateley, Source Books, Box 794, Trabuco Canyon, CA 92678.

"Remembering Your Heritage" from *Men Surviving Incest*, pp. 54–55, copyright 1992 by T. Thomas. Reprinted by permission of Launch Press.

"A Prayer to Move a Mountain" reprinted with permission from Abbey Press, St. Meinrad, IN 47557. All rights reserved.

First published in 1993 by Resurrection Press, Ltd.
P.O. Box 248
Williston Park, NY 11596

Second Printing – September 1995

Copyright © by Ave Clark, OP

ISBN 1-878718-12-6

Library of Congress Catalog Card Number 92-82000

Cover photograph and design by John Murello.

Printed in the United States of America.

Contents

ଓଃ

Dedication / Acknowledgments

ॐ

*"The wounded heart ... how strange a mystery that
God's most precious gift when transformed and healed
emerges as suffering embraced and celebrated as Resurrection."*

— A survivor – me

I AM A SURVIVOR OF ABUSE (incest, rape and sexual assaults). One cannot dare to say these brave,
painful words alone. One needs courageous and faithful companions to be with you in the terrible darkness,
in the many lonely and terrifying moments. One needs
great support to step forward and say: "I am a survivor, a valiant woman, a valiant man. I am a faithful
companion."

To all those persons who have believed in me, comforted me and affirmed me in my great fragileness of
mind, body and spirit, I thank you with all my heart
and offer each of you a loving rose with deep gratitude
and prayers of everlasting thanksgiving for bringing
me back to life and enabling me to celebrate life in
new and holy ways. There are many friends (survivors,
pro-survivors, professionals, spiritual guides and special friends) who have walked with me, stumbled with
me and wept with me. I have felt their deep compassion and respect. These faithful companions have held

me together, and still do, as I continue my journey of recovering from the deep wounds of sexual abuse.

In a special way I wish to dedicate this book to some very valiant and loyal companions without whom I would not have survived.

To my Amityville Dominican Community who supported me every day even when I was drowning in depression and wondering if I could ever be a sign of joy and hope again: I am deeply grateful for all the professional help they provided, for their companionship, prayer and friendship. I especially wish to thank Sister Veronica Greeley, O.P. (Prioress) for always believing in me; Sister Lenore Toscano, O.P. (Assistant Prioress) for her loyal friendship; and in a very special way, Sister Marilyn Breen, O.P. (Regional Director) for her extraordinary faithfulness and companionship.

To each of you, and to all my Dominican Sisters and friends: I thank you for always giving me a reassuring word and for stepping into a survivor's world of pain and heartache and helping to make it a bit more bearable.

To Dr. Frederic Gannon, M.D., psychiatrist of great compassion, gentleness, humor and faithfulness: I thank you for never giving up on me, for walking into my pain-filled, crippled life. Your courage and respect for me has enabled me to be a valiant and courageous healer, and to believe in myself again and again.

To all my friends who stood with me and cried with me as they tried to understand my struggles and pain: I say God bless you, I couldn't be recovering without such faithful and true friends.

To all the staff and residents of Villa St. John Vianney Hospital in Downingtown, Pennsylvania, where I spent over a year dealing with my breakdown and memories of abuse: I met Christ in all of you. I am especially grateful to Dr. Janet Connell, M.D., Dr. Eleanor Murdock, Ph.D., Dr. Martin Helldorfer, D.Min., and Kris Bowman, R.N.

To my cousins, Faith and Juliette: your coming forward to say, "We love you and want to be your friends and family" has truly been a healing force in my life.

To my brother Joe and sister-in-law Peggy: your hearts of love have consoled me.

To Bishop Rene Valero: your friendship and spiritual guidance helped me to find and keep a loving God in my darkest moments.

To all survivors: you have blessed my life with laughter, joy and shared tears and fears.

To those survivors who did not survive, who did battle with depression, deep anguish and dissociative disorders: I truly believe that the compassionate Lord is holding each of you tenderly in the palm of His hand. I know that you are all with me in spirit.

To all the children of the world: I hope and pray you feel loved and protected. We are all responsible for the wounded children of this world. We can be love for them — healing love.

To Sister Eva Mazzetta, O.P. who contributed her beautiful and courageous drawings to make this book a symbol of hope over evil, crime and sin: I thank you for your sensitivity and respect.

To my wonderful, dedicated and caring typists: I am deeply grateful to Sister Regina Rosaire Smith, O.P. and most especially to Sister Lorraine Mahoney, O.P. for her typing and helpful and caring suggestions for the final draft.

To the staff of Resurrection Press but especially to my editor, Emilie Cerar: I appreciate your taking a risk to allow a survivor to speak humbly from her wounded heart about her life and faith journey, her fears and darkness and still say, "This is a faithful and courageous woman." The opportunity you gave me has truly been a gift of grace for my healing and hopefully for other courageous healers.

To so many others that I hold in my heart (and to Monsignor Thomas Donovan for letting me run off tons of papers for all my drafts) with deep thanks for having walked so valiantly and gently with me in this sometimes stormy healing recovery process. Believe me, I feel your love and support embracing me and holding me up as a fragile rose of peace.

If I consider the rose, I must consider this:

> *The roots are the beginning of life;*
> *the stem represents my growing*
> *the thorns represent my armor*
> *The leaves are my happiness*
> *and the flowers represent my beauty.*
> *I have been hurt and*
> *just like the rose . . . I will bloom again.*

—Sister Ave Clark, O.P.,
Amityville Dominican Sister/
Adult Survivor of Abuse, January, 1993

Foreword

ᔥ

WHO AMONG US does not know something about sexual abuse? At last, the long sad silence which has surrounded it is being broken by valiant survivors like Ave Clark, O.P. Yet, we realize that what we do know is probably the tip of the iceberg. The statistics are overwhelming. One in every three female children, and one in every six male children in the United States will be sexually abused by the age of 18. In 85% of these cases, the abuser is someone known and trusted by the victim. Some claim that one in every three women in this country will become a rape victim. And researchers estimate that as many as 12 to 15 million women in the United States alone have suffered incestuous abuse. Many incest victims have been left permanently scarred by the experience.

We are beginning to realize that children whose innocence and trust have been violently betrayed tend to grow into adults plagued by an array of serious emotional and physical problems. As adults, those who have been violated as children frequently are unable to form intimate relationships. Many are overwhelmed by depression, guilt, self-hatred, sexual dysfunction, and self-destructive behavior. And all deserve our compassion, understanding, and encouragement.

Where to begin? This book is a particularly apt place

to start the learning of the heart necessary to sensitize ourselves to being better companions, healers and survivors of sexual abuse.

Ave Clark speaks from her heart in gentle yet compelling ways to uplift the spirit of the readers. Using poetry, scripture, imagery, and anecdotes, she paints a portrait of a courageous healer and invites the readers to recognize themselves in it. Poignantly and powerfully, this book also provides comfort and hope to those who have experienced the pain of sexual abuse in their own lives.

We read in Scripture the following words:

> *"I have set before you life and death,*
> *blessing and curse;*
> *therefore choose life,*
> *that you and your descendants may live . . . "*
>
> — Deuteronomy 30:19

Here is a book that helps the readers to choose life. It is sure to be a source book of hope to those who are intent on journeying toward wellness of body and spirit, and a reservoir of inspiration for those who are companions on the journey.

In her work with survivors and healers, Sister Ave Clark has become a guiding star, and in this book she has given all of us a sparkling gem. Thank you, Ave, for breaking your own silence so that the whole community may know the light and that we all might choose life.

— Gloria Durka, Ph.D.
Fordham University
Advent, 1992

LIGHTS
in the
DARKNESS

—— ☙ ——

Introduction

∞

THE ROAD NOT TAKEN

Two roads diverged in a yellow wood,
And sorry I could not travel both
And be one traveler, long I stood
And looked down one as far as I could
To where it bent in the undergrowth;
Then took the other, as just as fair,
And having perhaps the better claim
Because it was grassy and wanted wear;
Though as for that, the passing there
Had worn them really about the same,
And both that morning equally lay
In leaves no step had trodden black.
Oh, I kept the first for another day!
Yet knowing how way leads on to way,
I doubted if I should ever come back.
I shall be telling this with a sigh
Somewhere ages and ages hence:
Two roads diverged in a wood, and I —
I took the one less traveled by,
And that has made all the difference.

— Robert Frost

GOD CERTAINLY DOES LEAD US to paths we would not choose or ever dream we would journey — the paths of incest, sexual abuse and assaults speak of horrendous pain, devastating suffering and long-term aftereffects on a survivor's adult life. We must take the crooked and frightening path and believe that along the way we will meet caring professionals, support friends and special persons called "survivors" who understand us as we are ... women of courage ... men of courage ... valiant women and valiant men.

This book is for adult survivors of sexual abuse who have valiantly stepped forward out of the darkness of despair and anguish to discover healing lights of hope, comfort and faithful companionship. The journey for men and women who were abused as children or violated as adults is a journey of deep agony, heartache and loss. But for those who dare to take the journey to recovery and want so much to reclaim their lives in new and holy ways, it is and will continue to be a faith journey where struggle and suffering can be turned into blessing and gift as we survivors rediscover our inner goodness and recreate our lives, our world and our faith in valiant, heroic and caring ways.

This book is about how survivors face their pain and embrace deep wounds caused by sexual abuse and find caring and consoling companions to walk with them gently back into life. My hope, as a survivor who is still on this journey, is that as you read this book, you will no longer feel alone and you will come to believe that it is possible to survive and to celebrate your life and your journey to recovery.

This book is also for persons who minister to survivors of sexual abuse (incest, rape and sexual assaults) — for priests, religious, pastoral ministers, spiritual directors and friends. It is for compassionate ministers who walk gently along the painful road of recovering and reclaiming life with a survivor of sexual abuse.

Ministers need to understand the complex and painful issues of sexual abuse, the long-term aftereffects of abuse on the adult survivor's present life and the faith journey survivors need to take. Survivors need to feel the presence of Jesus' love and tenderness in appropriate ways in their violated, abused and traumatized lives.

There are four types of abuse: sexual abuse, physical abuse, neglect and emotional abuse. In this book I will focus primarily on sexual abuse. All the emotions evoked by speaking about sexual abuse can also be applied to the other types of abuse. Very often, a person who has been sexually abused has also endured (never accepted, just endured to survive) more than one type of abuse. Some of the terms I will use in this book will be explained briefly in the glossary.

I am writing this book as a survivor of sexual abuse who is coming out of the painful darkness of secrecy in hopes of bringing the tragedy of abuse into both society and church understanding. Abuse has been a source of agony, betrayal and pain that I have carried with me into my adulthood as many other survivors have done because of great fear.

Child abuse is a major social problem, a crime and a sin of betrayal against the sacredness of an innocent child's life. It casts a long, dark, horrifying shadow into adulthood; the fear, shame, guilt, depression, addictions and isolation many survivors experience is a relic of the past abuse. The saddest aftereffect of abuse is that it changes your life forever.

This book is not about struggling alone, but about feeling understood, learning ways to cope, and accepting and walking gently with a caring companion to reclaim and celebrate all of life.

Most of all, this book is about how we as Christians live out our faith by binding up each others' wounds with gentle compassion, respectful love and courageous companionship. If we are to follow Jesus, then we will be able to face the shadows of abuse that have stripped us of our dignity and perhaps we will be able to see the face of Jesus in a faithful companion who says: "I believe in you. Keep on. Don't give up." I truly believe that survivors are given the grace to journey into recovery and to trust in a loving God who will not abandon us in the unknown but will enable us to become courageous healers who will discover a new integrity called justice, a profound love called reverence and a new hope called faithfulness.

> *"A Christian is someone who shares the suffering of God in the world."*
>
> — Dietrich Bonhoeffer

May we be lights in the darkness for each other. May a new day dawn called peace, serenity and wholeness. May all people who have been violated find that the journey to survive is a holy opportunity to bless our world with what it so much needs, groans for and searches — community, solidarity, and healing.

Chapter 1

Valiant Survivors and Courageous Healers

 egin{center}CB\end{center}

S OMETIMES PEOPLE SAY "Why are you just talking
about this terrible incident *now* when it happened
so many years ago?" What people need to understand
is that sexual abuse is such an unbearable violation that
the victim blocks the memory — the terrible touch, the
terrible crime, the terrible sin, the unwanted and unholy
encounter that was too much for a small child's psyche
to understand. We learned a survival technique called
dissociation — numb yourself, go out of your body and
pretend it is happening to someone else. It is buried,
denied and ignored. But it is always there — hidden
deeply from the world, a silent pain that often goes
unnoticed and unattended for years and causes severe
emotional damage.

Survivors of abuse have been in hiding a long time.
Keeping the abuse buried deeply in their psyche has
caused many survivors to feel out of control. These are
some of the terrible effects.

- 90% of survivors have some form of an eating
disorder
- 90% of prisoners have a history of abuse

- 90% of survivors deal with some type of depressive disorder
- 85% of survivors have an alcohol or drug addiction
- 80% of homeless people have a history of abuse
- 75% of survivors have considered suicide
- 40% of survivors have attempted suicide
- 15% of survivors have committed suicide

Survivors trying to grapple with the long-term aftereffects of abuse in their lives sometimes feel:

- It's easier to eat or not eat to numb the pain.
- It's easier to drink and take drugs and forget even if only for today.
- It's easier to unleash your rage on others.
- It's easier to die than to live so painfully.

Ministers need to know some of a survivor's rehabilitation history:

- alcohol or drug addiction rehabilitation
- rehabilitation for eating disorders
- hospitalization for deep depression
- crisis intervention for suicide attempts
- divorce/loss of job/home/friendships

The minister can then understand somewhat the survivor's great need to build trust in a loving and caring God and in a minister. No easy journey.

I believe if some of the casualties of abuse had had more caring and supportive people to share the painful journey of recovery, they might have survived and found meaning in their life and even in their struggles — a second chance at living more free, caring and fulfilling lives. Unfortunately many cry inside: "I have no spirit; I am an unhappy person deserted by all but the grace of God." We live in a world where few people will dare to step out and be a Good Samaritan and risk getting bruised, frightened and perplexed by the human conflicts and wounded condition of others.

Some survivors with PTSD (Post Traumatic Stress Disorder) have to get in touch with a terribly damaged and disheveled psyche. Each day brings some trigger or event that rattles them with flashbacks and turns their world upside down and inside out. They feel as if they are on a roller coaster going backwards and they have to hang on to life without a seatbelt. These survivors have learned to live life more slowly than they would like to, keeping painful boundaries, taking medication and getting professional help.

Some survivors attend meetings for AA, ACOA, OA, EA and other self-help groups. They share their stories of failing, feeling defeated and giving up, hitting rock bottom, losing control, being in prison, in hospitals and rehab centers. All the wounded companions at the meetings listen without judgment or pat answers — only a fragile faith that says: *we care about you.* That is the grace of God in action.

Many survivors, like myself, have been hospitalized on one or more occasions. Hospitalization for an emotional illness is different from going to a hospital for treatment of a physical disease. The person experiencing the emotional disruption feels they are losing part of themselves and losing a hold on life. Everyone else is moving/doing/being while the person with the emotional trauma is just about existing. I have been in this frightening and scary space. It is filled with moments of feeling lost, forgotten and terribly abandoned, but being hospitalized helps the survivor to be protected when they are overwhelmed and shackled to the pain of abuse. Too often their hospitalization becomes another stigma in their life and in their recovery. However painful, survivors who have been hospitalized for emotional illness have done a courageous act by finding a safe space in the darkness.

Survivors need to learn to say *NO* (and mean it). They do not need to please everyone. They can respect their own personhood and protect themselves. *No* means that we have boundaries. When we were abused the sacred boundary of respect for our bodies, minds and spirits was broken. This broken boundary will take a lifetime to mend. We must believe that to be on the mend is good, holy and wholesome.

Companions on the Way

The dark shadows a minister will be confronted with are not easy ones to bring into the light. A survivor of sexual abuse feels the terror and is not able to trust that someone will take the time to understand. We sabotage recovery at times by acting smart or tough. This takes a lot of energy away from healing and recovering from deep wounds. Some helpful suggestions for ministers might be:

1. Listen carefully to the language of the survivor and respond to their "wretched journey," "dark pain," "lost hopes," with realistic hopes and prayers of comfort using gentle challenges and words of strength such as: "May the Lord give you the necessary strength and comfort this day to endure the wretchedness of this journey and help you to feel His peace and calm on a hard day."

2. Be respectful of the survivor's needs but do not feel you are expected to fulfill all their needs. Guide them to get involved in life. It is very easy to withdraw and hide the pain from others and end up in more pain yourself. Suggest self-help groups and retreat days for survivors.

3. Build up the survivor's self-esteem by acknowledging their creative and courageous steps forward and their innate ability to keep going. Some survivors use their gifts of art, dance and poetry to help others to heal. It might be a good idea to put some of these creative works into a church bulletin for others to reflect upon in their own journey.

4. Enable the survivor to let go of self-blame or any guilt for being abused. Help the survivor to learn to keep safe boundaries with abusers who still drag the survivor into dysfunctional loyalties.

5. Enable the survivor to see that their sexual abuse can be overcome and become a gift by sharing witness talks that give hope and deep faith that transcend the negative and celebrate life.

6. Encourage the survivor to have a broad support network — to find others to confide in, trust and

pray with — to offset their terrible loneliness and isolation.

7. Challenge the survivor in gentle, caring ways to say one, positive, good thing about themself every time you meet, e.g., I have a sense of humor, I am kind, I am a good listener, I can cry.

8. Congratulate the survivor on how they handled all the changes this journey has brought into their lives — changes that most of us would rather not endure.

9. If a survivor shares that they have some severe emotional and psychological addictions (suicidal thoughts, self-mutilation, drugs, alcohol or out-of-control eating or some type of sexual dysfunction) help them to find added support with a professional or treatment center. Let them know that you see that they are willing to fight bravely for their lives. Courageous people battle — they don't give up.

10. Be aware of any emergency that could evolve from a reaction to medication (seizures, blurred vision).

11. Most of all, celebrate, bless and praise the survivor's rediscovery of a God of hope, a God of great comfort and a God of great respect for them right now in their life. Pray with them — thanking God for their courage to unravel the dark shadows of abuse and asking for God's peace and inner healing.

Ministers to the abused need to focus on the positive side of all the struggles, dysfunctions and pain that survivors still battle. I see ministers and pastoral care workers as pilgrims of grace offering concern, hope and companionship — our cross-bearing companions — as we slowly conquer our fears step by step. It is the faltering steps on the road to Calvary that have always given me the most hope. When I think of the Stations of the Cross I wonder at the Station where Jesus falls the second time. Will he get up and if so, why? Just to continue on this terrible journey? Where is he going anyway, in circles into despair? And then at the next fall is where another human being helps Jesus to carry the cross.

A minister can share their own story of struggle as a means of saying, "I might not have been sexually abused but I can understand fear, disappointments, broken dreams and setbacks. We are all wounded in some way. By sharing your journey of healing the deep wounds of sexual abuse, I feel as if I have touched the garment of a pilgrim full of grace."

Praying with survivors prayers of affirmation and praise can be very simple, concrete and directed toward the survivor's own journey of healing.

- I affirm you in your struggle to give up — alcohol, drugs, sex, smoking, sweets, etc. (whatever the survivor shares as a struggle can be brought to the Lord in prayer and affirmed).

- I affirm you in your forgiveness of yourself and in overcoming your destructive ways.

Some survivors might want to work on forgiving those persons who abused them. This should be done with the help of a professional. It can be done personally in a face-to-face encounter with the abuser (never go alone), or it can be done symbolically by burning a picture, visiting a grave, or writing a letter and burning it. The affirmation and healing is to free the survivor of any guilt or shame that is one of the ugly scars of abuse.

Ministers can be companions of mercy, justice, peace, goodness, compassion and respect as they walk gently with hearts that care deeply for survivors who are stepping out to say *YES* to life and *NO* to abuse. These courageous healers are creating a more caring world. They have truly taken on the Risen Lord in all His glory — living life fully human and fully alive.

When we let God guide He will provide us with the necessary courage to make very hard healing choices. It's very important to be who you are in a bad space — sad, perplexed, frightened, etc. So remember not to compare yourself. Healing should not be a competitive issue but rather an enabling one. And what works for one may not work for others. Share suggestions and guides to inner healing that will enable the survivor to embrace the pain and discover the healing presence of God in their sacred space.

I encourage you to pray the scriptures together. To be assured of the Lord's presence:

- Psalm 9:9–10

- Isaiah 43:2

- Matthew 28:20

To be assured of the Lord's love:

- John 14:21

- 1 Corinthians 2:9

- 1 John 4:10

To be assured of the Lord's care:

- Psalm 55:23
- Philippians 1:6
- 1 Thessalonians 5:6–18

To be assured of the Lord's help in times of need:

- Isaiah 41:8–14
- Romans 15:13
- Ephesians 2:13–14

To be assured of the Lord's grace-filled guidance:

- Proverbs 16:3
- Ecclesiastes 2:26

To be assured of the Lord's companionship in this journey of recovering from sexual abuse is to befriend someone with an open heart, a valiant spirit and a faith that believes that compassionate love can heal and conquer unbearable pain and transform darkness into light — a light called faithfulness.

Chapter 2

Families ... of Yesterday

ੴ

O NE OF THE MOST PAINFUL ISSUES for a survivor
of sexual abuse is to deal with their family of origin. The people with whom the survivor, as a child,
should have felt protection, safety and nurturance instead felt abandonment, discord, rejection and abuse.
In Claudia Black's book, *Double Duty*, she gives us two
lists for survivors to reflect upon to help them see what
was dysfunctional in their family and what to strive for
in re-creating new, healthy and caring relationships.

In a nurturing family:

- People feel free to talk about inner feelings.

- All feelings are okay.

- The person is more important than performance.

- All subjects are open to discussion.

- Individual differences are accepted.

- Each person is responsible for his/her own actions.

- Respectful criticism is offered along with appropriate consequences for actions.

- There are few 'shoulds.'

- There are clear, flexible rules.

- The atmosphere is relaxed.

- There is joy.

- Family members face up to and work through stress.

- People have energy.

- People feel loving.

- Growth is celebrated.

- People have high self-worth.

- There is a strong parental coalition.

In a dysfunctional family:

- People compulsively protect inner feelings.

- Only 'certain' feelings are okay.

- Performance is more important than the person.

- There are many taboo subjects, lots of secrets.

- Everyone must conform to the strongest person's ideas and values.

- There is a great deal of control and criticism.

- There is punishment, shaming.

- There are lots of 'shoulds.'

- The rules are unclear, inconsistent, and rigid.

- The atmosphere is tense.

- There is much anger and fear.

- Stress is avoided and denied.

- People feel tired, hurt, and disappointed.

- Growth is discouraged.

- People have low self-worth.

- Coalitions form across generations.

Many people in recent years have come forward to share that they were brought up in an extremely dysfunctional family. The dark shadows of dysfunctional families hid, camouflaged and denied any problems, difficulties or abuse within the family and the family members learned to keep secrets, accept pain and bury their wounds. Some identify themselves as ACOA (Adult Children of Alcoholics). Growing up in alcoholic families has caused many of us to take on roles and to learn more dysfunctional behaviors just to ease our own sense of being overpowered so early in life. As adults we are enmeshed in extreme loyalties and excessive caregiving. We ache deeply to be an individual — a child of God. God forbid we should admit that we are in trouble and in need of help. Who will hear us or even believe us? We become confused and hide our true feelings, too scared or angry to come out with the words of truth that could help to free us. We become part of the dark shadows.

Very often life in an alcoholic family is shame-based. Some survivors of abuse were already immersed in a shame-based environment and when the abuse occurred it seemed as if this "were normal," "expected" or "deserved" behavior. "I was born to be abused," is what many survivors believe and struggle with. The worst part of being sexually abused as a child is that you were told this was good. What a confusing and frightening world to acclimate oneself to.

The pressures of life in our world are felt most profoundly in an ACOA family system and when one member within that system breaks the dark secret, cracks in the family picture surface and the hypocrisy is revealed. Sometimes people with ACOA backgrounds feel overwhelmed and stuck in a downward spiral of circumstances that seems impossible to reverse.

Survivors need to address their past with a trusted and caring companion ever so slowly. Burying or denying the past will only brew further agonizing issues. To look at what was and what should have been does not mean that we wallow in self-pity or re-abuse ourselves over and over again. If we can get in touch with these feelings and see how they have ruled us, then we can change a little bit at a time. Periodically, I catch myself slipping and then I dare to courageously say without blame or guilt:

I can be different today.
I can find a different way to respond to criticism,
    compliments and difficulties.
I can be my own person.

If a family is still dysfunctional and in denial, it is best for the survivor, as painful as this is, to set boundaries — communicate via the phone and keep a safe distance — while in the recovery phase of healing. Many families will continue their denial and even look at the person in recovery as the sick one, the weak one, the trouble maker, to keep at a distance. The truth often brings deep pain. If a family won't own its dysfunction, then for safety and healing, seek out other friends who will support you and be family for you. The family of yesterday cannot always help us to create a new tomorrow. We can never change our family, but we can change ourselves.

Families of yesterday created roles and even demanded roles of innocent children who somehow learned to accommodate to the adult's dysfunctional behavior in order to survive. Some of the roles that children had to bear were those of the overly-responsible child (hero, care-giver par excellence, little adult, parental-child), the placater (rescuer), the adjuster (lost or forgotten child, overly shy or timid), and some became the boisterous, acting-out child (scapegoat, loser).

The *lost child* sought solace in adjusting to a "bad situation" by ignoring it, denying it or pretending it didn't exist or that it didn't affect them. Just imagine the psychic energy it took to ignore being beaten, put down or even abused. So what appears as an easy-going attitude can really be a defense mechanism that keeps decisions, responsibility and creative ventures at a distance.

The *placaters* could get on your nerves without really meaning to. They want peace and will pay any price for it. They minimize their pain and are overly solicitous and sensitive to others. They put bandaids on everything and hope that no one will ever discover the deep, ugly wounds underneath — their own fear of falling apart, not being in control and worst of all, not being able to keep all the dysfunctional people happy. "Unreal" harmony is their goal and this is all done in the name of surviving more abuse.

The *acting-out child* or the *loser* in the family is probably the one who is closest to the truth and wants it to be known, discovered or identified. They just don't know the most appropriate way of telling the truth, so they tend to fuel the negative and this becomes their strength and their only way of getting all the pain and dark dysfunction out into the light. But their negative behavior is usually all that is seen and reacted to. Sad to say, those closest to the truth usually get involved in self-destructive behaviors (sex, alcohol, drugs, crime) that sometimes kills them. Very often they hold the key to dismantling the family dysfunction but they do not have the emotional resources to do so. They are the children that felt "too much," "too soon" and "too late."

Each of these roles has its strengths and its overwhelming liabilities. One of the issues that many survivors feel is that the strengths they have as adults were born too early in their lives at tremendous cost.

How Ministers Can Help

Ministers to the abused need to be in touch with family histories and the way the survivor dealt with the dysfunction in their life as a child. As the story unfolds, the minister will see the past being relived or overcome in the adult's present life. Confirming this in caring and gentle ways will help the survivor to slowly change, adjust or modify their behavior. This is how life can be lived and celebrated — as a survivor and never more as a victim. Companions can enable a survivor to look at how they are functioning at work, at home, and in the community and to assess their relationships. Do these relationships bring the survivor a feeling of joy or oppression, freedom or despair?

A survivor can be helped to identify their strengths and limitations and to surrender yesterday's roles to make room for healthy and creative roles and behaviors. A minister can enable a survivor who was once an overly-responsible child, a placater, a scapegoat or an acting-out child to refuse to be dominated, battered or abused any more. Survivors who can get in touch with the presence of love in their life can find healthy and holy solace in knowing that they now have the power to break any harmful control over their life. If survivors are to do this, even in small, everyday, ordinary occurrences, they need to learn how to:

- listen to their own needs without feeling selfish

- be honest with themselves

- believe they are special and unique

- find·people they can trust

- recognize rigid or unrealistic expectations of themselves and others

- find time to play, rest and relax

- place themselves in the presence of the holy and find deep comfort and companionship in the recovery journey

If we are lucky enough to have a family or even one or two members of our family who resonate with us in the recovery process — rejoice. Just accept. Don't try to force others into recovery; they have to want it for themselves. Family members who are not able to understand a person's need for safe boundaries, setting limits and feeling respected need to be kept at a healthy distance. Discover anew a family of friends you can trust and companions that seek to understand, to care and to respect you. The family of yesterday is gone. Stay connected to family members you feel safe with or create a new family of choice, people who want to be your friend, and who love you just for being who you are — a good person struggling to be set free of great emotional turmoil and pain.

Chapter 3

Pro Survivors

∽

PRO SURVIVORS ARE PERSONS who affirm the survivor's journey, who befriend the survivor in some helpful, healing way, persons who remain loyal to the survivor during a painful time, faithful companions, disciples of the heart, or as one friend said to me, just special friends who care deeply and want you to heal and celebrate your journey. We need these faithful companions in our corner rooting for us as we deal with the long-term aftereffects of sexual abuse.

Ministers, pastoral care workers and therapists are certainly Pro Survivors. They have stepped into an arena of deep pain and terrible human tragedy. Pro Survivors definitely need support in this bewildering time.

Ministers can be helpful to family members, community members, or close friends of the survivor by offering to be available to them and by listening to their fears and concerns of how the healing journey is affecting them. One of the most painful experiences of survivors is for a friend, partner, or family member to pull away or to deny the pain we are in. I now realize that the person pulling away is not able to enter into the pain of sexual abuse and share this vulnerable time. Perhaps it brings them too close to their own need for inner healing. Sadly we grieve these losses and in some way we understand their need for distance.

We have to learn to respect and accept other people's gifts and limitations in embracing a survivor's suffering and healing. We will discover that some relationships will change and some will dissolve. I usually share with survivors how to hold these people in their hearts and to gather the strength to meet new friends — helping professionals, other survivors and loyal friends who can embrace the healing journey.

Walking with a survivor will take you into places you would choose not to go:

- visiting a friend at a psychiatric hospital or rehabilitation center

- going to seminars on incest

- attending symposiums on the battered woman syndrome

- attending workshops on sexual abuse within the church

- attending retreat days for survivors of abuse who give witness stories of their abuse and survival

- going to conferences on dissociative disorders/ Multiple Personality Disorder

The companion needs helpful information that will enable them to validate their own feelings about abuse and how it affects a person's entire life.

Subscribing to newsletters such as the "NCPA Memorandum" (National Committee for Prevention of

Child Abuse) can be very helpful. Consider the following excerpt on "Adult Survivors of Childhood Abuse" from their November 1991 issue.

"Child abuse has lifelong effects. Adults who are survivors of childhood abuse often report a feeling of being 'stuck.' Their efforts to build and manage their lives often seem fruitless, hollow, or even hopeless. There can be a persistently nagging perception that they are somehow different from others.

"The adult symptoms of childhood abuse can take many forms:

- Difficulty in developing or maintaining close personal relationships.

- A strong desire to live in isolation or to 'hide out' from life.

- Physical ailments like neck, back, and stomach problems repeat and persist despite efforts at good self-care.

- Feelings of sadness, fear, and anger often seem unmanageable, even overwhelming.

- Panics, rages, depressions, sleep disorders, or suicidal thoughts interfere with efforts to reach cherished goals.

- Dependency on alcohol, other drugs, or food to buffer and cover feelings of humiliation, shame, and low self-esteem.

- Sexual problems like low sexual self-esteem, avoidance of sex, promiscuity, or an inability to experience orgasms or erections.

- Signs of trauma like panic attacks, numbing of body areas, and feelings of being disconnected from the body limit the ability to participate fully in life.

"Symptoms undisturbed for years may flare if a survivor enters a serious romance, considers marriage, or gives birth to a child. The intimacy and responsibility of a committed relationship may be feared. Caring for a child can arouse memories of unmet needs and lead to sadness and depression. Adult survivors may also fear that they will abuse their own child the way they were abused."

One of the best ways for persons supporting a survivor on their journey to healing is to be honest with what and how much you can handle. This enables the survivor to respect your boundaries as well as to identify their own.

It is good to talk to survivors about what helps them feel safe, protected and accepted when sharing about their journey. Very often survivors maintain a distance from persons, places or things that trigger their memories of abuse. Be respectful and aware of a survivor's need to feel safe. They might ask for a door or window to be open or closed. What might seem like a trivial or strange request to you is coming from someone who feels like a hostage because of their abuse. Anything that doesn't make them feel enclosed will help them. Tell them you appreciate their honesty and want to create a safe place for them — a sacred place.

It is also important for the companions to share with the survivors their need for sacred space and safe boundaries. It is a delicate balance. I have appreciated my support people sharing their boundaries with me. It helps a survivor to know that everyone is entitled to have their boundaries respected and also makes it clear that certain aspects of their journey need to be handled by professional and clinically trained persons. Survivors will admire you for sharing your gifts, limitations and boundaries with them.

As far as your time together goes, I suggest:

- a time limit on your visit

- an opening or closing prayer (maybe the survivor will bring one)

- an open invitation for a survivor to bring a comfort companion with them; this could be a doll or teddy bear or a heart pillow to hold or keep nearby or which they might ask you to hold during the session

Your respect and understanding of the comfort companions will enable the survivor to build a trusting relationship. They will feel deeply understood and free to share because you are sensitive to the outside world or family that did not offer them safety or comfort.

If a survivor is married, they might eventually ask if their partner could see you either alone or together with them. This is a very important step for the survivor. Very often the partner needs support in this journey as it affects their marital relationship. (See "Allies in Healing" in the bibliography under tapes.)

As a companion, try to get information about retreats offered for survivors of sexual abuse and suggest that this might help them in the spiritual part of their journey, but never say you "should" go to a retreat. It needs to be their decision and when they feel they can handle it. I guess you might say, in God's time. Sometimes partners of survivors as well as their spiritual director come to the retreats to listen to the witness talks. It helps everyone to hear how other survivors are attempting to go beyond survival.

We will never completely heal the wounds of our lost childhood or perhaps even reclaim all of our dignity, but we can learn healthy ways to cope, accept and work with the long-term aftereffects of abuse on our adult lives.

Sacred space is a gift we give to ourselves. A minister of love can be a great blessing in that space. How blessed we are to find a minister of love and to be a minister of love. Very often a companion will say to a survivor: "How blessed I am to know you. I have seen great faith."

Survivors can celebrate the persons who are journeying with them by writing a prayer to/for/about these special friends. Keep this list of names in a special place and carry it with you. Just the feel of a small piece of paper with meaningful names on it can get a survivor through a depressing or lonely time, i.e., holidays. Knowing that others truly care is a gift for healing. Friends come into our lives to share life — all of life. The good times and the bad times can be celebrated when a friend helps us to:

1. Have fun for fun's sake.

2. Talk about current issues in the news.

3. Go to a silly movie.

4. Ask for something you need.

5. Join them in social plans.

6. Pray for the gift of healing for both of you.

Be a caring presence for the survivor rather than trying to fix things for them. This enables the survivor to gain control and reclaim their autonomy. No matter how many support people a survivor might have, most of their healing time will be on their own. Just knowing that you believe in them can help them get through trying days and lonely nights of terror. It reminds me of Jesus in the agony in the garden. He asked his disciples just to come and watch. He didn't ask them to take on all his pain, problems, or anguish. Just your gift of presence can help someone work through some agony in their life.

Many of us are caregivers par excellence. We tend to get into jobs (ministries) that call us forth to take care of others' needs. In dealing with people who have been sexually abused, I think the best gift a minister can share is to tell people in recovery and their support people to respect each other's space, have realistic expectations and affirm the everydayness of life — to accept the ordinary and be grateful. Some simple guidelines:

1. Ask — don't demand.

2. Share — don't probe or intrude.

3. Respond — don't react.

4. Forgive — don't defend.

5. Pray — don't argue or ignore a difficulty.

I guess we need to be "very human" with each other and not be afraid to say we need help. A minister should be prepared to suggest professional help in a therapeutic setting to work out some deep-seated psychological problems caused by the abuse. Sometimes couples will need professional assistance in dealing with sexual dysfunction which might occur during the healing process.

No one person can take on all the healing that a survivor of sexual abuse needs. It would be too overwhelming. A minister needs to know their capacity to help a survivor and to share in helpful, sensitive and caring ways with professionals who support survivors. Otherwise we can end up being burnt out and feeling dismantled by the deep wounds caused by sexual abuse.

As a survivor I have deeply appreciated all those caregivers, helping professionals and loyal friends who have supported me. It has especially helped me to hear what they feel comfortable in sharing and in hearing. As a survivor I have learned to respect a healing companion's boundaries and limitations concerning abuse. Some of my greatest supports and comforts have been a phone call or card. I don't believe survivors need or want to have someone hold their hand 24 hours a day. That would be a crippling experience and cause co-dependency and block the growth of the survivor.

Belief in someone who struggles will be a mutual gift of belief. Knowing that you can be trusted and respected for who you are is truly a gift that calls forth life and affirms life in holy and wholesome ways. This is the love that Jesus asks us to have, "Love one another as I have loved you." (Jn 15:12) I call this a love of deep respect — Christian charity. What greater love than to lay down one's life for a friend in healthy, life-giving ways. In doing so everyone will discover lights of thankfulness, gratitude and joy invading our inner lives and spilling over into our communities, places of work and homes. Meeting a survivor can be challenging and at times quite confusing and even painful, but it can also have its grace-filled moments of celebration that enable all of us to walk together in harmony, gentleness and deep respect for our human condition. Ministers can offer prayers of joy, consolation, friendship and hope by joining with those who believe: "To struggle is not a disability, but to give up is." The poor, brokenhearted and abused are dear to the Lord — believe in them greatly and you shall know enduring love.

> *"How blessed are the poor in spirit:*
> *theirs is the kingdom of heaven."*
>
> —Matthew 5:3

Chapter 4

Pilgrims in Darkness

☙

IT IS TERRIBLY PAINFUL to witness the suffering of another human being. We tend to protect ourselves by some degree of dissociation. We remove ourselves from the pain or even deny it so that it does not enter our psychic world. We might do this automatically while watching some violent and abusive scenes on TV. You leave the room, change the channel or switch to another activity like reading a book or going for a walk. You can remove the unpleasantness and get on with your life with a more peace-filled feeling.

When someone is repeatedly abused, tortured or held captive, there is no physical escape. The person has no way to escape except through their psyche. In such traumatic situations, one learns to dissociate to an extreme degree — to go out of your own body while being abused. It's almost like a pretend game. Pretend it's not your body and then the abuse will not be your pain.

If a survivor comes to a minister and shares this experience, it is best to let the person explain it in their own words and not to ask too many specific questions. But what a minister can say is, "You had the inner creativity despite being held hostage to survive. You did say no to the abuse by dissociating from the unbearable violations."

Recently Marilyn Van Derbur Atler (the former 1958 Miss America) shared her story of being abused by her father for twelve years. To deal with the abuse she developed a day-child personality that accepted life and a night child personality that lived the horrors of being abused and held all the terrible memories. The night-child personality held all the bad memories so that the day-child could get on with life. Her sharing has enabled other survivors with dissociative disorders to feel less ashamed, alone, fearful and confused.

Dissociation is a survival technique. Many persons with dissociative disorders struggle daily to overcome fears of normal living that trigger them to dissociate. A minister should read some literature on dissociation (Multiple Personality Disorder) to understand a survivor who might tell you something one week and not remember it the next or who might change their personality or voice when sharing an extremely painful experience.

As a minister, you can learn to respect all the personalities within this courageous person. Different personalities were created to deal with the abuse, work, family dysfunctions and everyday life. Persons with MPD and dissociative disorder are to be affirmed, deeply respected and given gentle, caring reminders that these personalities helped this precious person to survive.

Multiple Personality Disorder is not demonic possession and a person with a dissociative disorder does not need exorcism. The media has sensationalized this disorder which is medically treatable. What these heroic survivors are daring to do, with professional help, is to integrate or enable their system of personalities to cooperate and live more peacefully within them. Needless to say, this is not an easy disorder for a survivor to live with. We lost something special, precious and sacred due to no fault of our own. Our abusers have sinned greatly. We need to sob, cry and weep deeply for the loss of our sacred dignity that was left dismantled, shattered, damaged and scarred.

A minister can gently listen to a survivor with MPD and recognize some deeply spiritual resources called faithfulness, hope and inner strength that reside within the individual. Tell them that you see and know them as a holy pilgrim journeying into unknown, dark places to reclaim life in new ways. The minister's affirmation and gentle presence will be a great healing gift on this journey into the terrible darkness to confront unspeakable evils and to discover one's own priceless pearl of goodness.

The minister who accompanies someone on this journey will find it a great faith journey. It would be so easy to ignore or deny the pain and the person but Jesus said: "Come, follow me. I will be your strength and your friend." Can we be the friendship of Jesus' presence on a road we never thought we would take? Perhaps it will be on this road less traveled that together we will discover the great meaning of compassion. To suffer with a survivor means we will participate in healing deep wounds and in bringing about a new and more respected world order — reverence for all of life.

Another loss to grieve is the loss of power. We lost it a long time ago when as a little child of three or four we were manipulated into being molested and abused. This was the beginning of our sense of being truly lost, helpless, and defenseless that increased over the years. No one was there to protect and defend us from the onslaught of sexual indignities that left us feeling worthless. Grieve the loss of power over your life that you lost so early and so very tragically. You lost the power to say yes and the power to say no. You were left in confusion. I believe it is a tremendous step to accept our powerlessness and then to celebrate its gift: to be deeply in touch with our vulnerability and to see the reflection of this powerlessness in every other person.

I have met ministers of compassion who have great courage. Very often, it has been a kind word, a simple prayer, a consoling note or call that has helped me to grasp the meaning of my struggle with a dissociative disorder. One minister gave me a Hallmark card that I put on my kitchen wall to read before I go to work, when I get home and on days my struggles and pain keep me housebound:

> I know God loves me
>   just the way I am,
>   but I also know He still
>   wants me to keep on growing and learning.
>   What can I learn from this day Lord?
>   Let me be open to you.
>   I am a miracle of God's creation
>   that's reason enough for me
>   to be today.
>   I'll do my best from moment to
>   moment and be thankful
>   to God for this day.
>   God's hand is always open

Today, let me put my hand in His . . .
in yours . . .

As ministers of gentle compassion you can enable someone who suffers from a trauma inflicted disorder to slowly and gently heal and find peace, calm, and joy in their wounded psyche one day at a time.

Many survivors like myself with dissociative disorders rejoice that we have found ministers in the church community who dare to grow in gentle understanding of our pain and deep wounds caused by sexual abuse. "I thank my God every time I think of you" (St. Paul to the Philippians). I believe that our loving God will help us to heal our broken hearts if we give him all the pieces.

There is no painless way out. But there is in this holy journey a sacred space that we will rediscover when we learn to trust again. The brightness of the light of love of others and of ourselves will invade the turmoil and enable us to hope and believe in the resurrection now. To seek resurrection actively is what the grieving process in recovery is all about. God offers us life. We can actively participate in the death/dying/and rising experience. We too can see a new light and be resurrection people. We are survivors — people moving beyond just surviving. We are "pilgrims of grace" daring to celebrate, share and bless our painful journey. We are faithful companions — joining with our brothers and sisters to establish a Kingdom where all of life is held sacred and where all of humanity meets and rises to new life at the cross. This is where we are each transformed and blessed as we help each other bear our burdens and turn our sorrows into joy as Jesus did. Alleluia.

I believe a minister can help a survivor slowly find a loving God in the chaos. This takes hard work. Recovery is not sitting in an easy chair, relaxing and closing our eyes to the world's pains. Recovery is painful. It tears us apart. All the illusions that kept us glued together and insulated us from the pain come falling down. We could not really touch another's pain because we had not touched our own deeply. We insulated our pain and numbed it in whatever way we could:

> Perfectionism
> Workaholism
> Being a Pleaser
> Caregiving Par Excellence
> Peace Maker
> Eating Disorders
> Alcohol
> Drugs
> Sex
> Hyperactivity
> Passivity
> — and the list goes on and on.

These are some of the ways survivors of sexual abuse deal with the reality of being violated in body, mind and spirit. The first step in recovery is to say first to yourself and then to a professional: "I am in terrible pain."

Some survivors write and make up poems about incest, rape and sexual abuse. Some survivors draw or scribble symbols all over an art pad to get out their imprisoned and anguished feelings of being attacked and destroyed. Some survivors dance or use symbolic gestures to share their pain. All of this is using creative energy to release feelings of great loss, to grieve and let go. It hurts a lot. A minister can set aside a time and sacred space to let the survivor grieve the worst pain. With comfort, respect and reverence I truly believe a survivor can feel God's loving and gentle presence in the chaos.

Is it possible to recover? Is it necessary to grieve so many losses? The answer to each question is *YES*, but don't do it alone. Find healthy outlets and good safe friends and trusted professionals to grieve with. As you journey into the dark rooms of recovery sometimes a great loneliness can overcome you. Stay connected to good friends via the phone, mail or get togethers. Find a caring companion who will not overpower you but who will help to empower you by recognizing your holy courage to enter into the recovery process.

A minister can help us celebrate, yes celebrate, not the pain of these losses but the genuine and authentic meaning that they can bring into our lives:

- refining us

- sharpening our awareness and need to have healthy all-embracing relationships

- enabling us to cultivate a greater respect for individual differences, limitations, gifts and graces

Have we really been given a gift, a holy opportunity to learn what mourning, dying and rising again are all about? Again and again we will hear the cries of our spirit seeking inner healing, not from our intellect but rather from our bruised hearts where suffering and vulnerability give birth to true joy even in a fragile

spirit. We need to grieve deeply, let go, and then celebrate what we have discovered on our painful journey:
that just as the grain of wheat must die to grow again,
so must survivors die to all that continues to hold them
in bondage. (See appendix for Litany for Grieving.)

Even as we grieve all the losses in the recovery process (different losses for each survivor) we will need
help in responding to these losses in self-nurturing, self-
loving and self-caring ways for our own sake. We can
make a commitment to grieve our losses when we are
brave enough to let go of our need to seek control and
power by caring for others' needs and forgetting our
own.

Chapter 5

Lost Childhood

ೞ

A DULT SURVIVORS OF ABUSE have lived their adulthoods so intensely because what they lost in their innocent childhoods seems to hold them prisoner from feeling free, independent, spontaneous or worthwhile. What they lost was their ability to trust, to feel protected and safe and to believe that they are able and deserving of enjoying life now, not just enduring it. Survivors of abuse were robbed of a precious and sacred gift — their childhood.

Ministers/pastoral care workers will see the adult survivor struggling to relax, to find peace and to search for comfort and support. Usually survivors weigh every word that is said to them. Does this person really care? Do they understand my embarrassing anxieties and phobias or do they dismiss them or put them down — or put me down? The battle to recover self-esteem is a long and grueling one for sexual abuse survivors who have known so much betrayal. When we were abused we heard:

> *You deserve this.*
> *You want this.*
> *You caused this.*

You enjoyed this.
You need this.

These cruel words said to a little child by people the child "trusted" stripped us of our inner confidence and gave us a terrible disbelief in others especially in adults and authority.

We always wait to have words that "seem" kind and caring to be turned against us. So no matter how many times we are told our work is exemplary or that our life is a credit to our ability to survive, we find a void inside — an empty, hollow, lonely void that no one can touch. We live isolated in a crowd, we cry ourselves to sleep night after night; we work very hard to try to feel safe on the outside and not let anyone know of our inner torment.

Where does an adult survivor go to discover the lost child within? How does one dare to reclaim some part of the abused little child and discover ways of celebrating the inner child? Carrying the secret has imprisoned the inner child who needs to be set free from the pain. We used tremendous emotional energy to wage a silent war inside of us. This left us with hardly any time to really enjoy life.

Ministers need to listen to survivors' stories and enable and encourage them to find ways for the desperate child within to be reclaimed and enjoyed. Adults who were abused as children very often had a "pretend" or phony laugh that only they knew. Today these same courageous adults can learn to laugh freely if they can see the present moment as a gift to be embraced. Little by little the self-conscious, serious, or frightened child will be healed, one day at a time.

Men and women who have sexual abuse histories have great difficulty in letting the child within feel joy or experience a carefree day without some hidden agenda attached to it. Just having fun for fun's sake is not easy for us. As children we were forced to take on adult roles, adult responsibility and fulfill adult needs and selfish pleasures well beyond what a little child's understanding or psyche could handle. We were the pacifier for someone's emotional and sexual needs. The little child was crushed and a detour out of childhood was taken. A minister who is in touch with their own inner child and their need for taking leisure time and enjoying healthy outlets will in some way be able to see the terrible paradox of an upside-down dysfunctional upbringing and its aftereffects on the survivor.

Ministers can enable a survivor to see the energy and creativity they have and to use the gifts that helped them to survive their torment, trauma and deep wounds in new nurturing ways. So often, this is the hardest step for a survivor of abuse. We are so used to looking outside of ourselves, assessing others' needs and taking care of others. To look within is painful but necessary for healing. "What do I need?" is not a selfish statement for a survivor of abuse. Write on your calendar: "this is your special day" and don't cross it out. It is very, very important to enjoy your leisure and time out with other friends. Ministers can help by sharing how their own need to take time out and have fun has released their own inner child. In some way we all need to let that child within gently come out of past darkness.

Seeing With a New Vision

Anyone who has ever been abused will bear deep emotional scars. Fear, anger, depression or addiction are detours to joy. Our perception of the world shattered by abuse distorts even our fleeting moments of joy, happiness and contentment.

One very important ingredient to finding a new vision is to develop a good sense of humor. Humor can truly be healing. It can lift up an aching spirit or a broken heart and alleviate our fear and anxiety. This is not a phoney humor but rather a genuine respectful humor that can enable us to laugh at ourselves. It can help us to find the silly in the absurd and it can bring us slowly out of the darkness of depression. Laughter can be healing. Survivors need to laugh more and take time to be silly, carefree and happy. Ministers can share moments of laughter with survivors and tell them that laughter and joy are the best medicine to reclaim a clearer vision of life.

A survivor needs to take time to be nurtured in order to see life with a new vision. Their body, their spirit and their soul are all in need of healing. A day at the beach, a walk in the park, a massage (if this doesn't cause flashbacks), some light reading, an ice cream cone — with or without sprinkles — or even a good health salad can be self-nurturing. Survivors deny their personal needs and take care of everyone else's needs, getting so involved in one activity or cause to the exclusion of other healthy outlets. We need a variety of activities to help us to heal and to move beyond the pain that sometimes pops up at unsuspecting times during a survivor's day. If one takes time and sets aside special carefree moments to relax, rest and stay calm, one will slowly rediscover that "fun" can be very healing and will help when the clouds or shadows of abuse come by.

Do the simple, ordinary and extraordinary play things with friends who deeply care and understand. We can help to set each other free — free to celebrate your inner child. Today you, I and all survivors deserve great love and tender moments of stepping out of our pain and living life anew. So:

- blow bubbles

- swing on a swing

- build a sand castle

- hug a doll/teddy bear

- buy a rose ... or pick a yellow dandelion

- get in a rocking chair and curl up

- play some gentle tapes

- pray with your heart

- watch a funny video and listen to your laughter

- call a friend

Some survivors choose to develop the spiritual aspect of their lives through days of prayer, reflection and meditation and time spent getting to know a Lord of peace, joy and hope. If we are to heal, we must take care of all aspects of our lives — emotional, psychological, physical and spiritual.

Survivors of sexual abuse can rebirth their lives over and over again one day at a time. A survivor can rebirth life when they feel themselves slipping into self-destructive behaviors by going to a group meeting or by calling a sponsor or a friend. A survivor can rebirth life by seeking the guidance of a professional to set healthy and appropriate boundaries and limits so that one can find peace and joy. A survivor can rebirth his/her own life by daring to witness to what we think is the worst tragedy that could ever befall a human being . . . the loss of one's dignity.

It is here at this sacred moment that we will ever so gently and gradually be lifted up by a loving God who does not want us to just endure life but in some mysterious way to bear witness to the joys and sorrows in life. This will be the power of our witness: when we come to realize that in some way our life's journey to recovery can make a difference — that all of life is not in vain — all of life is intertwined. One who dares so courageously to bear witness to the suffering in their life can come to know true peace, joy and compassion in deep and profound ways.

It will be here that our wounds and scars are healed, comforted and transformed into blessings . . . blessings that set us free to meet the pain and be healed and become a faithful companion for another survivor.

"A friend loveth at all times."
— Proverbs 17:17

This will be a very hard journey and require lots of hard work for the survivor. They will need lots of support, affirmation and encouragement from others who care. Looking at the world through rose-colored glasses is not real, but looking at the world with a clear vision of life will enable us to see hard truths, and to reassess how we respond and what we can do to make the world more humane, more caring and more compassionate.

Seeing with a new vision will enable us to break the victim mentality and provide us with new ways of living, coping and dealing with the long term aftereffects of sexual abuse. People in recovery are gifted with a holy opportunity to be transformed and to see life in new and holy ways — all of life as gift to be celebrated.

A PRAYER TO MOVE A MOUNTAIN

Lord, I have a mountain in my life — You know which one — the one I keep trying to climb, time after time, and keep sliding back down, humbled and discouraged. . . . This mountain is so high I can't even see the top. . . . Looking back though, I see so many other mountains I've climbed, only by Your strength and wisdom. . . . Even though this one seems to be the worst one yet. Help me to trust and fully believe that You know the way over, and that someday I'll look back and wonder, as with all the others, where my climbing faith was. . . . Amen.

Chapter 6

Survivors of Rape

☙

"Come to me all you who are burdened and I will give you comfort."

— Matthew 11:28

WHAT DOES ONE SAY to a person (man, woman or child) who has experienced rape? There are no words and too many words. There are silent words and rage-filled words. There are confused words and concerned words. There are words of the heart — tender, compassionate, respectful, listening words.

Rape is a violent, selfish, inhuman act of terror. It leaves the victim shattered, frightened and causes many deaths, the major one being the death of trust. No longer is the world safe. Eyes bewildered become hypervigilant and just wait — wait to be hurt and plundered again and again.

It is a terrible crime motivated by an attacker's need to show their power or to express anger against another person. The crime is no respecter of age or gender. Its roots very often have been planted early in a person's life where love or respect and feeling safe and protected were denied. Sometimes a person who has been emotionally damaged themselves equates love with hurting, abusing or controlling another and feels

51

no remorse with this inappropriate and harmful behavior. The victim holds it all — feels the shame, the guilt, the rage, the emotional problems, stress disorder, phobias, depression and flashbacks. Who will listen? Who will help us to heal? There are so many of us.

- Ten women are raped every hour.

- One in eleven men are sexually assaulted.

- Ten percent of all rape victims are under age 5 — usually attacked by a family member. This is incest.

- The untold, unrecorded numbers of victims of rape in war.

- Sixty percent of rape victims experience post-traumatic stress disorder and 16% still suffer with emotional problems 15 years following the rape.

The minister should be aware of the terrible after-effects of rape and also see rape as an act of violence, a crime and a terrible sin against the body, mind and spirit of an innocent child or adult.

A person who survives rape has to have tremendous courage — a courage that still struggles with a wounded psyche that remembers. Very often a survivor can get through months and even years, before the impact of the rape pops up with a terrifying fury — with feelings of insecurity, low self-esteem, depression, nightmares and panic attacks. One wonders if it is possible to put one foot in front of the other and appear normal any more. Rape damages not only the psyche but the very soul of a person — their human dignity is often shattered. One could call rape a barbaric experience of soul murder. To embark on the healing journey with a survivor of rape will be an extraordinary journey of tremendous courage and faithfulness for both minister and survivor.

The victim is terribly damaged physically, emotionally, and spiritually. Victims usually withdraw from any activities that were previously life-giving and joy-filled and develop debilitating stress-related disorders and phobias if they do not get professional help. The terrible trauma of rape will follow the victim through life causing out-of-control anxiety and pain-filled anguish.

Very often, after a person shares that they have been raped, they re-experience the trauma and all the shame connected with it. If this person is an incest survivor, there will be the added trauma of their childhood abuse. Sometimes you will hear that this hurtful behavior went on for years.

A minister may not be ready to handle their own shocked feelings when someone reveals that they were raped. The victim's emotional turmoil can pull at the very fibers of their own frail humanity. They might feel the stress of the victim and the ache and pain of their wounds. This is why it is very important for a minister to know and understand the effects and aftershocks of being sexually abused and to set realistic boundaries on how much they can handle.

A minister can respond in a non-threatening manner which both can handle. The first thing to say is: "You survived. At the time of the rape you were a victim, but today you come forward with great courage. You survived a deeply cruel act of selfishness and terror. You are truly valiant and heroic. Your struggle to reclaim and nurture your life can truly be a blessing for you. Be not afraid, I'll walk with you *gently* on this painful healing journey. Like Jesus, you have experienced an agony of darkness. I respect you. You have courage." We need to hear this as we have felt powerless for most of our life. Anyone who has been raped and dares to share the trauma is usually asking for and looking for comfort and support to keep on living and wanting to live more joyfully.

A minister can gently *listen* and share that they deeply care. It will not do any good to keep telling the person to look at all the good they do until they can learn to feel good inside. It's the inner spirit that needs healing. It cries out to be healed of an undeserved wound.

Ask the woman/man if they would like you to offer a prayer for surviving such a terribly damaging experience. The best prayers of comfort and compassion come from a deeply caring heart filled with great respect. This helps the survivor to feel believed in, respected and cared for as a good person and not just as a person filled with shame and guilt.

Ministers of compassion can offer to read a meaningful poem or a passage from scripture that will enable the survivor to hold the still victimized part of their life up to an all loving and all embracing God. Some examples are: *Poems from Mantras from a Poet ... Jessica Powers* by Bishop Robert Morneau and sacred scripture: 2 Corinthians 12:10, John 1:5, John 8:32, Isaiah 43:1–2.

Men and women who have been sexually violated have lost part of their sacred space. You can invite a survivor to take time to re-create that space in new and healthy ways and you can do that re-creating with them as a faithful companion. Just being a kind, caring listener with great compassion, validates their experience, affirms their goodness and acknowledges their tremendous resiliency. Tell them you *believe* in them and want to journey with them to heal this dark wound and find some light of hope, comfort and joy to share with them. Just knowing that someone is willing to listen and allow us to cry can enable a person feeling victimized to let go of the pain and hold on to the courage and faith they need to progress in their recovery.

It is also helpful for some survivors to keep a journal called "Steps out of the Darkness." This is a healthy way to reclaim their inner goodness by remembering the lights of hope that they discovered in the darkness. This can be expressed in written words, drawings or just a word or two. It can be a reminder to the survivor of the steps they have taken so courageously to heal. Congratulate yourself for every step you dare to take. Here are some suggestions:

- Take a fun walk and notice all the beautiful colors in the world.

- Buy a rose . . . just for yourself.

- Go shopping . . . with no money and be able to laugh at all the packages you didn't bring home.

- Call a friend . . . just to chat about the good things in life.

- Go to a funny movie and *listen* to yourself laugh.

- Practice keeping healthy and safe boundaries for yourself and don't worry about what others think.

The minister can also help the victim to become a survivor and be self-directed even in the small, ordinary steps of overcoming or dealing with panic attacks. Asking the survivor, "What do you need to help you?" can seem confusing to them since they often buried any needs they had just as they suppressed the trauma. Now, they will also be uncovering needs and this can be scary too.

Reclaiming our inner goodness when we feel so shattered can seem an insurmountable task. The survivor might wonder if it is possible to unravel all the trauma and pain and emerge whole. I know you should never attempt to unravel this alone. Perhaps instead of trying to move a mountain of pain we can learn to climb the mountain together and find paths of hope, faith and love along the way to comfort and support us.

Allow the survivor to share how the rape has affected their relationships/family/church/work with no judgments, no shoulds or oughts. Ask the person who was raped if they have had professional help in dealing with the trauma of being violated. Would they see a group experience as helpful or do they feel more at ease in a one-to-one sharing? One should never be forced into something they cannot emotionally handle at this vulnerable time in their life.

As a survivor, people have shared with me about being raped, abused and terribly violated. I can feel their pain and terror. I tell them I care and I will never give up on them. Believe, believe with your broken heart, wounded spirit, and shattered psyche that you can embrace this pain but don't do it alone. And to ministers of compassion I say, pray with/for survivors a prayer from your heart such as:

May the light shine in your brokenness;

Let peace be at your side in knowing others care and so does the Lord;

May we find mercy and compassion to embrace us in our suffering and may we walk gently in healing;

Let us celebrate this moment of a faithful companion's valiant journey to see Jesus reflected in their inner goodness;

I care ... go gently ... you are heroic. I won't give up on you. You are more than your brokenness. You are a light in the darkness. May we gather strength for the journey together ... to see Jesus in one another's suffering and to behold the face of God.

In *Trauma Recovery Publications* by Dr. Joel Brande, M.D. there is a wonderful outline of 12 spiritual steps to be used with/by survivors of trauma.

TWELVE SPIRITUAL STEPS

One: Power vs. Victimization. We admit that we are powerless to control victimization and the destructive use of power and seek the help of a good higher power (God as individually understood), to gain positive power in our lives.

Two: Seeking Meaning. We seek to discover meaning in our traumatic experiences and look to God, as individually understood, to help us find meaning.

Three: Trust vs. Shame and Doubt. Burdened with distrust, shame, and doubt, we seek God's healing and help in order to trust.

Four: Self-Inventory. We acknowledge to ourselves, to God and another human being, our short-comings and shameful secrets. We seek his help to heal our shame, accept our positive qualities, and change our negative ones.

Five: Anger. We seek God's help to understand anger, control its destructiveness, and channel it in constructive ways.

Six: Fear. We seek God's help to relinquish 'the wall' around our emotions and his protective presence during moments of terror and risk.

Seven: Guilt. We seek God's help to face guilt, to make amends when possible, to accept his forgiveness, and to forgive ourselves.

Eight: Grief. We seek God's help to grieve those we have lost, face our painful memories and emotions, and let our tears heal our sorrows.

Nine: Life vs. Death. We reveal to God and someone we trust all remaining self-destructive wishes and, with his help, make a commitment to life.

Ten: Justice vs. Revenge. We seek God's help to pursue the cause of justice, to gain freedom from revengeful wishes and plans, and for a desire to be channels of his forgiveness to those we once hated.

Eleven: Finding Purpose. We seek knowledge and direction from God and surrender ourselves to his leadership in order to find a renewed purpose for our lives.

Twelve: Love. We seek God's love in our lives, to help us renew our commitment to friends and family, love those we have found difficult to love, and help those who have been victims as we once were.

What a wonderful gift of grace to be able to be a pilgrim in the ruins, to feel the anguish and heartache, and to offer a healing word, a comforting touch, a respectful silence. What a wonderful gift to be called a disciple of Jesus. I have met some and I thank God for them.

> *Disciple of Jesus, weary and silent,*
> *aware, in the darkness of challenges*
> *failed longings unfulfilled,*
> *remembering the passion that sent you forth*
> *young and bright, and fired with hope.*
>
> *Disciple of Jesus, weary and silent,*
> *world unchanged, its darkness still deep,*
> *dreams dispelled and visions blurred,*
> *How is it now with you?*
>
> *Trailing behind me the sparkle and fire*
> *of early passion,*
> *bruised and tender from love's long thrust.*
> *Now is the finest, greatest moment*
> *and now the ultimate death.*
>
> *For I, Disciple of Jesus,*
> *to stand before my God,*
> *weary, silent, and all alone,*
> *claiming only, "I was there."*
>
> —*I Hear a Seed Growing* by Edwina Gateley

Chapter 7

Survivors of Suicide

Cʒ

*To all the children who survived but most of all to those
who didn't, I pray, "May flights of angels sing thee to
thy rest."*

PEOPLE ASK WHY, WHY DOES someone take their
life? How could they do such a terrible thing? How
could they do that to us? Yes, we survivors of suicide are
left with many unanswered, painful questions. What
did I miss? Didn't I see how down my friend was? Well,
of course I did. I'm right beside her with all my desperate feelings, anxieties, phobias, depressive episodes and
even suicidal thoughts. But I am still here. My friend is
gone. My friend is dead. The despair of being so sad,
so frightened, so angry, so out of control, so alone, so
useless, damaged and worthless, has pulled my friend
to the last moment when the lights dimmed never to
be reclaimed.

Why, why can't we save each other? Why am I still
wanting to save my friend? I don't think she really
wanted to die, but she wanted the pain to die. Suicide
is the final act of a desperate person clinging hopelessly
to life and embracing death as the terrible solution to
abuse. It is a tragedy, not a healing solution.

The memories of being so very young and vulnerable, so trusting and dependent cause the adult survivor dealing with the aftereffects of abuse to feel guilt, blame and repugnance at themselves. The pain is turned inward and twists us into a spiral of downward depressions, debilitating a person's spirits and self-esteem to a zero position in life. Why? Why go on? Who cares? I don't. I can't take this pain anymore. No one knows the secret that tears us apart inside, festers and crushes us. Some survivors run from activity to activity, going in a vicious circle as a subterfuge. Some strike out and keep others at a distance because intimacy is seen as harmful.

Sexual abuse shatters us forever and we scatter within in various ways to gain some control: eating disorders, alcohol and drug addictions, sexual promiscuity, sexual dysfunctions, hyperactivity, hyperalertness, insomnia, physical pains and emotional turmoil wrack our bodies, minds and psyches. You name it, some survivor will have it. Turmoil lodges deep within us until an explosion, an earthquake called breakdown, takes place. Then, hopefully, we get professional help to guide us on the dark, ugly journey of disclosure (and confrontation for some) and dealing with our chronic illnesses and terrible, dark thoughts of giving up.

The road that sexual abuse creates for survivors is riddled with chaotic darkness, out-of-control fears, rage and anger to such a degree that one is sometimes driven into violent behavior against themselves and others. It is a terrible way to live. We need to give support to others who battle the collapse of their spirits and lift them up so they will not be among the 1.5 % of deaths listed as suicide.

How can we help someone who is so frantic, so despairing, so down and out? If someone is sharing terrible, dark, suicidal feelings with you, tell them to stay connected to friends and other survivors and to go to a professional counselor. Have them go to a hospital emergency room and tell them you are in a dark moment. Sometimes you will be admitted for your protection. Some survivors are hospitalized and learn techniques to recognize and tell others about their suicidal thoughts.

Companions must learn to recognize the signs of confusion and despair. Sometimes these signs are well camouflaged and hidden by the survivor of abuse. They feel ashamed of these feelings and try to push on. Mental illness becomes the second battle for the survivor to deal with and dare to survive. It seems to the distraught survivor that suicide is a choice — a horrible choice to end it all, to at last rid yourself of the pain, agony, depressions, and addictions.

We are all called to reach out to the broken hearted, the oppressed and the abused and to truly love as Christ did — to bind up each other's wounds. A minister can tell the survivor to write down what is so painful — too painful to say — and then to bury it, discard it, burn it, or tear it up. Do this symbolically. Tell the survivor that the feelings and pain need to be gently released and removed. Be with them as best you can — a call, a card or a get together. Tell them you can feel their pain, rage and agony. Usually a survivor with suicidal feelings is looking for others to help them to care again.

Despite our best efforts, a wounded spirit may sink into a very dark moment — so close to the edge. But if they are aware of the ragged and zig-zag path of recovering from sexual abuse, just maybe they will believe enough to say: "Please save me." Hopefully someone will be there to say: "I will care for you. I want you to live." Then we can pray that the gentle presence of the Lord will bring the needed peace to the survivor — lifting them up on wings of eagles.

I cannot say enough to church ministers about recognizing the signs and symptoms of despair — listen with your heart and communicate your caring for a struggling survivor. "Keep on, don't give up, push forward. You deserve more of life and less of pain. I value you. I value the courage it takes to seek recovering from such deep wounds. You are a courageous person." Tell them *now.* Tell someone coming to you for comfort, healing and advice that you reverence the space they are in and will walk with them. No one should ever feel that they don't count and that their pain is too heavy, that no good could ever come of this turmoil. Believe with them that out of chaos can come new life. Believe with all your heart and soul that you can break open the word of Jesus' promise to bring *all* to new life. It has helped me tremendously to meet ministers of love who reverence my struggles and help to push me forward and let me know that I am not alone.

How I wish I could bring my friend back. I can't. I am now a survivor of suicide with many, many sad and confusing thoughts. Can I make it? I am so fragile, so fearful, and I too suffer from chronic, agonizing depressions. Will these dark feelings kill me too? I've been on the edge, on the rim, on the cliff, overwhelmed and crushed in spirit. I call. I cry. I tell someone if I am feeling suicidal. Please don't let me be lost forever too!

Survivors of suicide and survivors of abuse have to walk in and out of tragedy and somehow not let it ruin the rest of their lives. We can choose, we can decide to heal, to celebrate and to embrace the suffering and find meaningful ways to live with hope for ourselves and others. We can learn very slowly to let go and let God guide us with companions who remain steadfast and help us to reclaim, rebuild and rediscover love in the ruins.

With time, tenderness and the gentle compassion of companions we will be able to hold ourselves together, to move a bit farther away from the edge, the rim, the awful darkness of the cliff called depression. I cannot say this loud enough — don't keep those feelings bottled inside yourself. And to those who care, don't take someone's deep pain lightly. They survived this far, but will they tomorrow?

IS THERE A TOMORROW?

I learned to fear at an early age.
I also learned to hide fear; but
     it lurked just beneath
the surface of my thin facade of all is O.K.
I learned to hide deep inside
     and slowly I lost the light of day
          and submerged I became
     in deep, deep darkness
called despair . . . it's not O.K.
But cries I heard . . . a spirit
     wept, crawled and sobbed
          to be delivered

Yet fear, fear weighs us
 down,
   even in this
     New Year . . . alas,
   the journey to go on . . . Is that O.K.?

— Ave Clark, O.P.,
Adult Survivor of Abuse
January 1, 1993

(written after a terrible dark bout of depression
and yet . . . still trying and clinging to being just
O.K. . . .)

Chapter 8

Healing of Abusers

ೞ

P EOPLE WHO ABUSE are very sick. They are in need of long-term psychiatric treatment and spiritual help. Very often men or women who abuse have backgrounds of abuse, dysfunction, neglect or violence. This in no way gives any credence or validity to their destructive behavior. Abuse is always wrong. It is a crime against an innocent victim and a sin that cries out for repentance and restitution by the abuser.

Someone who is abusing a child, battering a wife or seeking unhealthy outlets for their own suppressed agony may at some point confide in a clergy person or pastoral care worker. The necessary ingredient is compassion for the abuser but with a firm stand against the continuation of their destructive behavior.

A good video or other resource can help someone who is trying to unravel their violent tendencies and might enable them to understand their need and obligation to seek professional treatment. (See bibliography for available tapes.) Some people who abuse will try and get in touch with why they have become involved in such perverse and destructive behavior but very often they will not seek treatment or counseling until the abusive situation has been publicly exposed through the media or legal proceedings. Some abusers have no remorse or feelings of guilt concerning the abuse. They refuse to see anything wrong in their behavior. This is indeed very hard for survivors, who are experiencing the debilitating aftereffects of abuse on their life and relationships.

Men or women who abuse usually do so to satisfy their own unmet emotional or sexual needs; some even commit unbelievable acts of violence and torture that lead to the murder of innocent victims. Very often these violent abusers feel no pleasure in these encounters, but they release the violence inside of them in cruel, unspeakable acts. Some of these violent abusers are psychotically demented, lacking any conscience or responsibility for their heinous crimes and studies indicate that some of these people have brain dysfunctions or lack a chemical in their brain that controls aggression, rage, and uncontrollable sexual urges. These people need serious medical treatment and sometimes removal from society to safeguard themselves and others.

The abuser is usually fixated on a child because of their own abusive and neglected childhood. Some abusers are pedophiles and seek out children of a certain age. This is often a key to discovering that the adult abuser is still emotionally fixated at a much younger level of development. These abusers lack control. Their lives are often filled with guilt, anxiety and fear of discovery. They learn to camouflage and shield themselves from disclosure. They learn to hide their abusive behavior by appearing extremely responsible in certain areas of life; they become overachievers in whom vulnerable souls feel they can confide. Most abusers are not strangers to their victims. In fact, many of the men or women who abuse are people to whom others turn for help. Their secret is so hidden that the unsuspecting victim is unaware of the trauma they are in danger of experiencing.

People who abuse come from every strata of our society, from all races, creeds or vocations. People who have abused need help — professional help and spiritual help. They must take responsibility for their inappropriate behavior and violent tendencies. They are on a crash course to self-destruction in continuing abusive behavior and others will continue to suffer unjust pain and terrible inhuman indignities until they are stopped. Since abuse (past and present) is a crime, it has to be reported to the legal authorities. Survivors who make the decision to confront or to take legal action against an abuser will need lots of support. This is another step in their own healing journey that seeks justice. Very often an abuser cannot accept the idea of being imprisoned or being remanded to a rehabilitation facility.

I believe that people who abuse others by violating another person's body or spirit need to be confronted but not in a vindictive manner that continues the cycle of dehumanizing another human being. Yes, we need justice, but we also need to restore decency to our inner spirits, and to be able to inform the proper authorities in a confidential and caring way that will enable us to reclaim hope for all who are involved — the victim and the abuser. It is far better to confront an abuser in a nonviolent and compassionate way so that all persons can experience some healing. If the proper authorities are prompted to investigate reported abusive incidents, I believe that the cycle of abuse will lessen and our society, churches and homes can become safer and healthier places in which to live.

If a person has an abusive history, it is very important that they be honest and open to the proper authorities so as to insure a safe place for them to work and minister. Abuse histories need not be boulders in a person's life but if the behavior has been judged addictive, then guidelines for future "safe" work and ministry need to be implemented to safeguard all persons, including the person with the addictive disorder.

A person might have abused someone and then realize the gravity and wrongness of their behavior and seek counsel and ways in which to change this behavior. If a person can truly come to repentance and meet with the person they abused and ask forgiveness from the person they have harmed, then this can be a healing moment. We need to recognize that the abuser is seeking healing of their past behaviors. A person needs to feel affirmed for this step. In cases like this, it is best that all people involved sit down with a counselor and make a decision to report or not to report the incident. However, it is very important that the person who did the abuse, monitor their behavior and keep in touch with a counselor.

I do believe as a community we must learn to forgive and respect people who take the painful steps to change inappropriate behaviors. No one needs to be reminded over and over again of their shadow side but rather to be affirmed for their steps into the light of finding healthy and appropriate ways to express feelings and affection. If we want someone to heal, then we have to walk with them gently and with respect.

Communities of faith can be a valuable and healing

resource to offenders, survivors and support persons touched by the horrors of sexual abuse. It would be wonderful if our churches could openly offer vigils or days of healing for abuse victims, offenders and survivors. How can we ever heal if we can't bring all this pain to a place of sacred compassion?

Abusers are human beings — broken and tormented in many ways. Their violence and assaults on other innocent persons can never be accepted, condoned or hidden. My hope is that ministers will be direct, confrontational and supportive to those men or women who dare to come forward and say: "Please help me. I am abusing a child, my wife, my student, my neighbor, my parishioner, my patient." Men and women who abuse have probably suffered from their acts of abuse in hidden and debilitating ways. Secrecy breeds all sorts of illnesses. We all have a shadow side and very often as we deal with persons who have become abusers we are brought face to face with our own vulnerability and our need to control and to hide our insecurities. If we can see a reflection of our own weakness that could get out of control, then we will dare to walk with abusers and to speak the truth and find justice for all. I feel it is very important that ministers listen with respect and also with an educated concern that the only real cure for a person who abuses is to stop the behavior and get psychiatric help with lots of follow-up and support. Be compassionate — love the sinner but hate the sin.

I have met some abusers who have suffered deeply for the acts of abuse and violence they forced on their little sons, daughters or adult victims. They are skyrocketing into other addictions, depressions and dysfunctional behaviors to cover up the pain and humiliation of what they have done. This pain can follow them all through life until they meet someone who does not condemn them as a person, but says with great concern that they need to get help to change. They need to hear that you will walk with them in this painful journey, and will call upon the Lord who lifted up the most wounded sinners seeking forgiveness. This is a long road with volatile feelings and excruciating shame.

> *The Lord is my shepherd, he gives me all*
> *He takes me where the cool rains fall.*
> *He is the place free from earthly strife.*
> *He gives me help, he gives me life.*
>
> —Psalm 23:1–2

Abusers can seek life instead of death — life to be lived with great respect for another and even for themselves.

Chapter 9

Sacred Betrayals

CR

PEOPLE WHO HAVE BEEN ABUSED are vulnerable people who very often seek the comfort of professionals, ministers, or pastoral care workers on their journey to heal deep wounds. A person who shares their vulnerability needs to know that the person to whom they turn for solace, advice and comfort is a person with moral and ethical beliefs. These beliefs hold all people sacred no matter what condition they are in. Persons who are involved in counseling people suffering the anguish of sexual abuse need to keep boundaries, set limits and provide a role model for the survivor.

Unfortunately, this is not always the experience of a survivor who dares to step out and seek healing. Sometimes they come in contact with someone in a healing profession who violates their ethical responsibility to provide safety, respect and dignity and the survivor is once again escalated into a victim role and feels broken and dehumanized. A sacred trust is broken by a small percentage of doctors, clergy or pastoral care workers. The professional loses sight of their own dignity and does a terrible disservice to another human being. They not only abuse their office, authority or ministry; they also misuse their power and degrade their own state in life.

This experience for survivors has many devastating effects. Why, why this second layer of abuse, a sacred betrayal? No one is without guile, without a shadow side. All of us are capable of evil and we are all capable of compassion. We choose to empower people or we choose to overpower people. Sometimes a person uses their ministry in ways that are not healthy, holy or life-giving. This is what happens when a person loses sight of who they are in a particular role.

The pain of such an experience is so shattering to a survivor that they very often end up discounting any good in other professionals, clergy or caregivers. They cut themselves off from others who could help them. Unless one can reclaim one's own personal power and dignity, the imbalance of power is forever to be a victim.

To whom can these survivors turn for solace, validation and support? One only hopes that they believe enough in themselves to get away from such harmful relationships and tell someone. The violation by a professional is a very serious crime and a heinous sin. It definitely destroys a trust relationship and any healing that took place. The survivor must start all over again. Is it possible for them to ever trust again?

The news media daily reports stories of professional, clergy and school personnel abusing children. This has heightened people's awareness that anyone is capable of abusing, violating and using other people — even children — for their own emotional and sexual needs. We must educate children and adults to respect each other's boundaries, to affirm each other's dignity and to never intrude on someone's sacred space.

It is never okay to abuse anyone. It is our responsibility as caring ministers to compassionately respond to someone who shares this deep, emotional and humiliating pain. A minister should let the survivor know that in no way was this abuse their fault. Let the survivor know that they will be protected and deeply respected by them. Talk openly about boundary issues. This will help the survivor to believe that they can trust you and also feel safe.

Very often, when a church person is involved in sexually abusing a child or an adult, the image of a loving God is also shattered or even lost. A faith crisis is set off that will probably take a lifetime to reclaim or to heal. Ministers need healthy outlets. Ministers need to balance their ministry involvements and need significant relationships outside of ministry. If a person is so absorbed in ministry and does not take time for leisure, friends and solitude, it is easy to lose sight of the ethical and moral ramifications of their professional call to serve others, not to be served by them.

Institutions such as the Church can speak out and say, "We care that someone hurt you." This takes great courage, humility and faith. When a Church member fails in their responsibility to another member, we should not shroud it in secrecy or parade it publicly, but rather deal with it. Offer the survivor of such abuse compassion, listen to them, validate their story, and get the abuser the professional and legal help they need before another person becomes a victim.

Ministers need to be in touch with their understanding of justice. Some survivors might choose to talk to the legal authorities about being sexually abused by a professional. Hopefully, the survivor will feel supported in this heroic endeavor. Usually, what they truly want is not media coverage but compassion by those who are in authority and can help to stop the harmful behavior. No one else must suffer such an indignity — a sacred betrayal. There has been a conspiracy of silence in families about child sexual abuse. There has also been a conspiracy of silence in Church and society. The silence has usually protected the abuser and forgotten the lost ones — the victims who struggled in the darkness.

Survivors have often carried the burden of keeping the silence until it finally broke them and their relationships — even with the one they most needed and wanted — God. Dioceses, chanceries, church councils all over the United States are now taking heroic steps to condemn any type of abuse and especially abuse by church professionals. We cannot bury this pain, we must bring it to the light in compassionate and caring ways. It will not be easy. It is time to speak the truth and help our society and our institutions to mend and to change any dysfunctional behavior which controls and manipulates. We can create a more caring community when we see each other as human beings with limitations, needs and a sacred dignity. We need to respect everyone's need for healthy space, quiet time and healthy relationships that call forth life. No one deserves to have the very core of their inner spirit dismantled or mishandled. Trust builds hope. Abuse destroys hope.

At the November 1992 National Bishops Conference the Bishops set forth a pledge to share compassion and pastoral concern for persons suffering from sex abuse caused by Church persons. The points included:

- Responding "promptly" to allegations of abuse.

- Suspending priests "promptly" in cases where there is reason to believe the allegations are true.

- Reporting incidents to civil authorities and cooperating in their investigations.

- Dealing with the emotional and spiritual crises that such cases cause to victims and their families.

- Dealing as openly as possible with members of the community on the matter, without invading the privacy of victims and their families.

Perhaps in coming together to address these issues, we will heal some deep wounds in our society and in our hearts and learn to love one another as Jesus did — to give from hearts that truly love, respect and celebrate life as sacred, reverenced and blessed. Companions who journey with a survivor through sacred betrayal can truly be a blessing and provide a sacred space for this unbearable pain and lift up a spirit to a blessed space called healing.

Chapter 10

Survivors Among the Clergy and Religious

 C3

THE DEVASTATING STATISTICS that one in three girls and one in six boys will be abused before the age of 18 is no secret. Many of these boys and girls will grow into adulthood suppressing the terrible travesty of human violation, feeling the deadly silent pain inside and sometimes hiding it in very exhausting and painful ways.

It is not surprising that some of these men and women end up in caring professions. Very often if one cannot heal their own pain or deep wound, the next best thing is to help other victims. Many survivors in the mental health and social service fields serve others' needs while burying their own. Some therapists who have been abused are able to facilitate excellent groups because they know the pain and the need to find a safe space to reveal their secrets.

We should not be shocked to realize that some religious and clergy persons have also been victims of sexual abuse. They very often feel like tarnished fixtures or phonies in the Church they serve. I speak as a Dominican Sister, who has served the Lord faithfully for thirty years. Over the past five years, my secret, my hidden piece of dirt, started leaking out of me: depression, PTSD, dissociation, fear, nightmares and eventually a breakdown leading to a psychiatric hospitalization. Even now I feel like hiding or disappearing so I would not have to face the world, my community or even myself with this dark secret, but somehow I do want to live and grow and so I have decided to speak the truth as a Dominican whose motto is "VERITAS." It is not easy for a survivor or for a community to come to terms with this volatile issue.

Very often the tortured survivor in church service feels so bad about themselves that the only way to possibly measure up is to be *very good* in ministry and that often means burning out. If you don't speak the truth and tell the secret, there is no rest.

Survivors of abuse in religious life are no different from survivors who are single or married. All of us suffer the long term aftereffects of abuse and the aftereffects will spill over into our family life, work life, married life, community life and church service. If one goes away to "rest and recuperate" and is never able to free oneself by addressing their painful past, then what takes place is a secondary denial experience — one feels that it isn't "good" to tell. It won't sound "good" or look "good" for anyone. It ends up that you are forced once again to role play an even greater tragedy — to keep the truth to yourself as an adult. But we can redeem what we cherish if we speak the truth and break the silence.

The Church is a "sacred" home where all are welcome to pray, to serve and to heal. Survivors of abuse should not feel less worthy to come to this sacred home to pray, to serve and "be healed." Living in community is just like anywhere else. People are real, human, limited and gifted. Some will be able to understand, walk with you and support you. It can be an opportunity for the community to get in touch with its "heart." When communities learn how to respond to deep wounds inside their ranks, they can become wounded healers, not just people who serve but people who follow Jesus right to the cross. Very slowly a transformation takes place. We really become disciples of the Lord — loyal Dominicans, Franciscans, Jesuits, etc.

Men and women religious have shared with me their fear of revealing their history of being sexually abused. I can't tell someone else what they should do. I can only ponder with them and suggest that perhaps there is someone in their community that they could go to. It's what I call "selective" sharing. It enables someone in great pain to start to create a healing circle of support. I am very "selective" with how much I share with others since it is a very emotional issue and everyone needs to feel safe. I have spoken to men and women across the United States, Canada and Europe in all states of life — married, single and religious. They are good, holy people who choose to remain in their vocation and courageously struggle to reclaim and rediscover their own inner goodness. We are all faithful companions.

I no longer put my head down at community talks on the vows or feel that I am less a religious because I was abused and violated. Perhaps I need to hold my head up and believe a little bit more that I am a good, holy and worthy religious woman. My heart goes out to other religious men and women who have taken the journey to speak the truth. These courageous healers need your support, affirmation and deep respect. To community and diocesan personnel I say: "Love each other intensely from the heart," (1 Pet 1:22) because this sister, brother or priest speaking the truth is doing so not just to unburden their own pain but so we can become more compassionate and deeply committed ministers of the church, wounded but gifted with an enduring love. "It is together in Christ that we will give glory to the Father of Our Lord Jesus Christ, and be of one heart" (Rom 15:6).

As members of the Church we all need to get in touch with that which holds us imprisoned and be freed. What better place to do it than in a sacred place where we can embrace our personal poverty, anguish and oppression. This is a holy place. Solidarity is the reality of human existence and its first hope is for survival. I have survived to speak the truth because of my solidarity with my Dominican Sisters, because they cared and loved me so much — not just my accomplishments and good works, but they also enabled me to see that my deep wounds could be transformed and shared as "VERITAS" for others.

THE ROSEBUD

Stifled, enfolded
bound up within
So I first came to you
Blush of red seated
on dull rustic green.
Thus you selected me
Fragile, so frail
fearful yet strong
You lifted me up —
what joy, I belong!
With new life astir
I knew I was free
To give, to receive,
to be a new me.
With petals untethered
my beauty I saw,
A rose in full glory
love-warmed through the thaw.

—Sr. Maria DePaul, S.S.C.M.

Chapter 11

Spiritual Aftereffects of Abuse

CƷ

"Abused heart, it should not hurt to be you.
If it does, remember that I am with you
in all your hurt and shame. Your life
will be understood someday."

— *My Heart's Journal*

I CAN REMEMBER as a little child begging God not to let the abuse happen again. But it did. I used to wonder, does God hear me? Sometimes I would wonder, if God is everywhere then why does this terrible encounter with an adult keep happening to me. Did God close his eyes, was he repulsed, angry or just as frightened as I was? I used to talk to God in between my sobs and say, "Why God, why me? Where are you God?" Such was a little child's world of words and her belief that God wouldn't stay where something disgusting, harmful or dirty was taking place. The little child learned early to feel the guilt and to own the blame that she did not deserve, but such was a little child's world. She even blamed herself thinking that God had closed his eyes because she was not a good, holy and clean child, but a little whore. I now know God didn't close his eyes. Somehow the God of my abused child came into the lonely darkness and the child found a God she called friend.

Many survivors can reclaim their image of God by giving God a name that would not remind the survivor of their abuser. How can a survivor call God a "father" when her memories of a father are of incest. (The same can be true if the abuser is a brother, uncle, grandfather, priest, male doctor.) Somehow a survivor needs to see God in a different light — not an almighty judge or an all-powerful ruler. A survivor can give God names that will enable them to feel God's presence as gentle, caring and consoling — not pushing us around or pulling us apart but rather enabling us and lifting us up with compassion and great respect. Ministers can invite a survivor to list positive names for God: Companion, Comforter, Fellow Sojourner, Gentle Star, Pilgrim Friend. These names can give the survivor an opportunity to keep or discover God in their life and to feel a presence of the holy and sacred for their deep wounds.

Men and women who have been sexually abused will sometimes blame God for their abuse. God should have saved us. Some survivors have very strong negative feelings towards God. If God is all-powerful, then God should have and could have stopped the abuse and the violence. Over the years, I have come to realize the God of Silence was right there, next to us, not blaming us and not throwing more guilt on us. He feels every pain and holds it with us. The God of Silence waited years with some survivors to help them to realize that the abuser made bad choices that were not of God's loving plan but of man's selfish exploitation. I also believe that God cried with us.

If anyone wants to truly minister to a survivor of sexual abuse, be prepared to shed tears or feel deep pain for/with the survivor. There will be a long continuum of "God experiences," including ignoring a God-presence in one's life. This journey with God must be respected. Sometimes in the great absence of God one is able to get in touch with deep meanings and realize that their spiritual development was attacked and shattered at the moment of abuse. The God of an abused heart does not want the man or woman who suffered the indignities of incest, rape and sexual assaults to be alone anymore. The God of Silence is also a God who has brought us to a safe and sacred place, and to a safe and trusted healer to whom we can unburden our aching hearts and wounded spirits. The God of Silence who walked with us when we were fearful, depressed, addicted or despairing is enabling us to gently and safely speak the truth that will set us free. God is also going to walk with us as we recover and reclaim a voice that will at last be heard.

Many people in recovery call upon a Higher Power. I believe this is a spiritual way of getting in touch with our need to reclaim and discover a loving, spiritual presence in our lives. We learn slowly, ever so slowly, to trust a power greater than us — greater than any man or woman's power to control. It is a power that transcends the pain of sickness, death and violations of human rights. It is a power that is not destructive, harsh or judgmental. It is a power — a spiritual dimension that we gradually come in touch with as "the holy." I believe that ministers to the abused need to be in touch with the philosophy of AA, 12 Step programs and self-help groups that many survivors attend. Ministers can affirm the survivors in their journey to trust a Higher Power, a spirit called "the holy."

Very often, survivors will only want some recognition of their spiritual side without what I call heavy duty spiritual encounters. It can turn away someone who is looking for a spiritual connection if they feel forced. I truly believe God waits patiently for those of us with heavy hearts and crushed spirits. God invites us to come as we are — bruised, wounded and fearful — and his love is enough for us.

Church ministers can truly enable a survivor of sexual abuse to take spiritual steps out of the darkness. I suggest reading the serenity prayer together to help both the survivor and the minister to realize that healing will take place when we create a sacred space for pain, deep anguish, mental illness and all the other aftereffects of abuse — a place where the holy and the unholy can meet and mend deep wounds.

THE SERENITY PRAYER

God grant me the serenity
to accept the things I cannot change,
the courage to change the things I can
and the wisdom to know the difference.

I will never believe that God wants us to suffer any indignities, especially the indignity of sexual abuse. I do not believe God causes wars, tornados or bridges to collapse just to test our faithfulness or to see how strong we are. What I do believe is that the God of Creation groans as he sees how men and women mistreat the earth, the animals and the material resources meant to be shared by all, not hoarded by a few.

I believe that the God of Love is feeling the victim's desperation and degradation when rape, sexual abuse and bodily assaults are endured at the hands of selfish and sick people called abusers. I believe a God of gentle compassion is calling us forth to create a new world order in compassionate words that reach out to those who suffer from poverty, oppression and violence and bring a sense of peace, hope and harmony back to a very broken and wounded world. God created us to know and to share his love with each other. He gave us a precious gift to choose to love and not to abuse children; to choose to respect, not to demean or violate women; to choose to respect all people no matter what their race, creed or color. We can choose. We are given that great, holy freedom. God is not to blame.

Our image of God might have been broken, shattered and dismantled when we were being abused but I truly believe with all my inner strength and with my fragile spirit that God's love cannot be destroyed by any abusive act, no matter how violent. We survivors just need holy guides who will dare to take the zigzagging spiritual journey of recovery from sexual abuse with us. Then we can begin to reclaim and rediscover an image of God that reflects decency, joy and an innate goodness.

> *"Those who walk blamelessly and do justice . . .*
> *shall never be disturbed."*
>
> — Psalm 15:2, 5

Chapter 12

Praying When Troubled

❧

TO PRAY IS TRULY A BLESSING. What a survivor needs to do is to pray out of deep pain and brokenness, deep anguish and depression, deep trauma and hopelessness and know that God blesses these prayers. If we read the Psalms we will be able to identify our feelings with those of the psalmist who called out to the Lord in great suffering and sorrow. The Lord Jesus himself felt great sorrow in Gethsemane when he said to his apostles: "My soul is very sorrowful; even to death..." and later he fell down and prayed. I picture his prayer as prayers of groaning, moaning and tears falling silently but painfully down his face, onto his body and into the earth. Have you ever cried so much and prayed so hard for comfort and understanding that you fall down — perhaps only in a psychic way? You just hold on to life with your fragile hopes and your innate though wounded trust in the Lord's guiding presence.

One of my surviving techniques for dealing with insomnia and night terror is to say a survivor's rosary. I call it my "ten mercy beads." My prayer on each bead is:

Lord, walk with me.
Lord, be gentle and help me to be gentle with my pain.

Lord, show me your mercy in the ordinary events of each day.

Lord, help me to rest and stay calm.

Lord, fill my emptiness with your presence.

Lord, comfort my aching spirit and help me to comfort others.

Lord, let me close my eyes and sleep in peace.

Lord, teach me to take time with myself.

Lord, be my constant and loyal friend.

Lord, help me to be valiant.

This rosary of mercy can be said with a companion. We have within us a resiliency to tolerate great sorrow when we know others care about us and pray for our healing and wholeness.

One cliche that should never be used with a man or woman trying to heal the deep wounds of sexual abuse is, "to offer up this suffering." I think a healthier way to handle any suffering, especially suffering that was unjustly inflicted by another, is to learn to deal with it by acknowledging the cruel and unfair intrusion of pain and to unravel it in caring and respectful ways.

Prayer can enable a survivor to embrace the broken-ness in themselves, in others and in our world. Prayers of broken hearts can be heard even in the dark silence of abuse. We can dare to pray in uncomplicated and very human ways. We can cry out prayers out of our wounded spirits — prayers that dwell deep in the silent spaces of our pain, where no voices are needed, only "tender trust." Maybe this is where we learn to discover the faithful resiliency of our fragile spirits that so courageously survived sexual abuse. Perhaps it is here that we are able to embrace the God of silence and draw on his strength in adversity, his acceptance of a cross that so cruelly abused him and tore his humanity apart. In this silent space we can learn to listen calmly to the healing moments of prayer rendered humbly and with dignity for hopes of rising to new life. Praying with a survivor can help them to pick up their battered bodies, shattered psyches and in some sacred and gentle way move beyond the pain. I think it is a terrible waste of time and human energy to try to make sense out of being abused. It will never, never make sense. What we have to do is to set our hearts on the road ahead and forge forward ever so heroically to reclaim our lost dignity.

"The Lord hears the cry of the poor, blessed be the Lord," is a refrain from a song about oppression and suffering. We are told prayer lifts up our hearts and minds to a loving God. Is it possible to lift up the wounded spirit of an abused heart and fragmented soul? I believe so, if we can allow ourselves to be awkward, wounded, broken — in other words, to drop the mask or facade of what we want others to believe — and to let go, let go, let go.

Praying for courage takes great humility. I have prayed that God would give me the courage to live through frightening flashbacks and then to gather myself with God's grace to step out into life as a sign of joy and hope for myself and for others. We need lots of support to do this. Sometimes survivors arrive at God's door wondering: "Will he hear me now as an adult survivor of childhood sexual abuse? I am grown up and the weight of the abuse can no longer be endured without some inner peace, without a holy companion on this dark journey." A compassionate minister will em-

brace your pain in a quiet, respectful way — a sacred
way called prayer of the heart. True prayer has a heart
and no words need to explain its deep love.

Some of the Psalms a companion might share with a
survivor of abuse to heal a broken heart and wounded
spirit are the Psalms that cry out and search for ways
out of injustice, war, famine and violence. One is Psalm
107 where a survivor can reflect on the Lord's great
faithfulness as we stagger through the grueling healing
process. The author Graham Greene once said: "The
kind of faith that issues from despair is one that speaks
of a heart and spirit that has been tested." We must believe that in the face of adversity, depression and illness,
one's faith can be strengthened. It does not have to be
lost. Perhaps it is only in the desert and wilderness experience that a flower of great holiness and gentleness
can appear as a sign of new life, hope renewed and
love shared.

God is not looking for pious prayers but deeply
faithful prayers. These prayers of faithfulness are the
prayers of those who cry in the desert, the wilderness of illness and darkness, the emptiness of feeling
abandoned, rejected and misunderstood. Perhaps with
ministers of love we survivors will be able to grasp the
height and depth of God's ever-abiding love. God's love
embraces our fragile trust and enables us to slowly surrender the pain, anger, rage and despair of a bruised
body and spirit and to find sacred silences where only
a God of mercy, a God of compassion and a God of
goodness can dwell. We can only hope to attain this sacred moment by letting our prayer be very human and
very disjointed at times. Sometimes our prayer will be
empty and we must believe that the God of enduring

love will fill up what is wanting in us. A companion can learn to wait with the survivor — to wait with a faithful heart — for it will only be in God's time that the season of healing, called reconciliation, takes place and bears fruits of joy, acceptance and consolation.

If anyone thinks that this healing is a peace-filled journey, it is not. Quite the contrary, it is bumpy, rocky, terribly painful and lonely. Great trust will be needed amidst great breakdowns. Great hope will be needed amidst terrible, debilitating despair. The God of compassion understands the prayers of those who are troubled. He understands the prayers that are riddled with anxiety, fear and lost dreams. This God hears our prayers and lifts them up to be blessed with new life, new hope and great consolation. The very silence of God is his invitation to gently heal and walk back with us into life, even into the shadows, and discover gifts of faith, hope and love.

Prayer is not mere words but the very fabric of our life; how we live, respond and care about ourselves and others is a prayer. The greatest guides to me have been those persons who walked beside me and shared their own faltering prayer of incompleteness. The greatest gift we can share with others is our humble and very human prayer of being God's presence in faithfulness. God's presence is a trusting relationship and God's presence is very simply — loving one another as Jesus did — with great compassion.

> *"As a heart longs for flowing streams*
> *so my soul longs for Thee, O God.*
> *My heart is ready, O God, my heart is ready."*
> —Psalm 42:1, 108:1

Chapter 13

Valiant Men Joining Valiant Women

ଓଃ

F OR FAR TOO MANY YEARS the secret of sexual abuse was hidden and locked in a very wounded psyche and fearful spirit. Slowly and painfully many women started coming forward and at last were heard and validated by mental health professionals. Pain, terrible, unbearable pain was unburdened and the journey to healing was begun.

In the shadows of women coming forth are the male survivors of childhood sexual abuse. One hundred thousand male children are sexually abused each year and it is estimated that one in six men are sexually assaulted in their lifetime. Boys are more often abused by an older male who is not a family member though incest by a family member is also present in the stories of male survivors. Frequently it is someone who is trusted by the child's family: a neighbor, a school or church person or other authority figure who uses their position to inflict sexual violations upon an innocent child.

It becomes overwhelming and very confusing to the male survivor to sort out the mixed messages that illicit sexual encounters had on their early childhood. Why, why would I attract a man? This leaves a little boy terribly alone, confused and usually with massive emotional upheaval concerning his own male identity. So the secret is buried and creates a broken and humiliated center within the young boy.

If the young boy was abused by a woman — a mother, aunt, grandmother, teacher, nurse, or other authority figure they were sometimes told that they were special and very lucky to have this "loving" experience — this is *our* secret. The young boy did not feel special inside; just utter disgust, hurt and humiliation that this should be happening. So, better to keep quiet.

Male survivors who courageously come forward to share their dark secret, do so very cautiously. I have been in groups where grown men have sobbed out their story of sexual abuse and how the silent torture robbed them of years of happiness and healthy relationships. Some men took to drugs, alcohol, and workaholism like many women survivors. Some ways were destructive and others were creative but what they all felt inside was the aching question: "Why, why me, what was wrong with me that someone would want to have sex with a boy? Why couldn't I stop it? Boys are supposed to be strong!"

Our society has too many false images, ideals and perfect scenarios that survivors of abuse have had to hide behind: real men don't cry, weep, sob or show emotion; real men hold themselves together; real men never get abused — that's for sissies. If you aren't strong or in total control, then you are a wimp or a loser and you better go out and prove yourself somehow. It's time for us to realize that all of our children (boys and girls) are vulnerable to being abused. Boys and girls need to be taught that each of them must respect each other and in return respect themselves. No one deserves to be abused.

Men and women survivors have many of the same feelings: fear, rage, anger, anxiety, depression, self-doubt, confusion, low self-esteem, addictions and chronic disorders and illnesses. Some male survivors also deal with a terrible hate of their sex and a terrible uneasiness with the opposite sex.

People who have been sexually abused early in their childhoods have had to struggle with closeness, warmth, and intimacy, always fearing that some sexual act would be demanded or forced upon them. This feeling has an overriding effect on work, relationships and a person's inner spirit. Everything is held "at a distance" or everything is rigidly controlled and manipulated to hide the pain and heinous events of the past. Men and women survivors can offer each other a relationship that can be tender, affectionate, respectful, empathetic and genuinely caring with no sexual expression expected.

The cycle of abuse learned early in childhood is very often triggered in adult relationships, sometimes causing abused male adults to get double messages from women. A man needs to know he *deserves* a healthy, life-giving relationship that is mutual and not self-serving. No man deserves to be demasculinated. In genuine, mutual relationships one discovers themselves as unique, sacred and worthy of a love that celebrates life. It is a tragedy that male survivors have been lost in the shadows. They need to be validated, supported and affirmed on their heroic journey to heal the deep wounds caused by sexual abuse.

Like women survivors, some men will develop eating disorders, especially overeating, to cover up any likeable part of their body. Some don't eat and fade into the woodwork of life, hardly seen and hardly heard. The same is true of alcohol and drug addictions. These chemicals are overused to relieve or put a clamp on the volcano of feelings caused by being sexually abused. Men also turn to other addictive substances (cigarettes, candy, coffee, running) to numb or deny their pain. Needless to say, they become their own victimizers and end up with dysfunctional behaviors and unhealthy relationships and an array of other painful aftereffects that slowly dismantle their lives.

Some men and women who have been abused perpetuate the cycle of abuse by molesting innocent children. We can stop this terrible chain of abuse by speaking the truth to them, acknowledging their pain and letting them know they did not deserve it and it was an unlawful use of power. They need to hear: "Today you can change this chain of abuse and acknowledge your inner torment and release the rage with a caring professional and other survivors who will validate your journey and help you to heal inappropriate behaviors such as sexual compulsions, chemical addictions, male-role confusion, and relationship dysfunctions. Just as you dared to try to say no to the abuse when you were young, today you can say no to abusive behaviors towards yourself or others. You have to really *care, respect* and *love* yourself to get better."

One of the saddest and cruelest aftereffects of child sexual abuse can be venereal disease and AIDS. Others can also become victims of horrifying and death-threatening illnesses (drugs, alcohol, self-mutilation, eating disorders, chronic depression, psychotic behavior, and eventually suicide).

Male survivors need just as much support as women survivors. They, too, are mending deep emotional scars that have damaged a large part of their lives. I am truly grateful for meeting these valiant men and I hope that they know that others will walk with them out of the shadows to discover and reclaim their lives and be comforted in knowing that their own inner strength has gotten them this far in their recovery.

We must allow all men to be human and show tenderness, affection and deep feelings. If men are sad, then they should cry. If men have been abused or victimized, then they should be able to seek consolation and comfort. The strongest men I have met are those who can cry, weep, sob and feel deep pain. I have met these men in a group for survivors of abuse. Most often they are outnumbered by women survivors but dare to join valiant women for the journey of healing they are embracing, often with double shame. What will people think of a man who has been abused?

The adult male survivor is a real man who dares to risk and share that sexual abuse was part of his broken childhood and still holds him victim in certain aspects of his life. This is the reason he dares to speak. He, too, is valiant.

Ministers of healing, especially male ministers, can truly be a gift to a male survivor (in some cases a female minister will be a healing companion to a male survivor) to offer comfort, consolation, friendship and respect for a man who needs to heal and reclaim his masculine dignity. At a young age, a little boy's role model was distorted and broken; it truly becomes a

blessing to learn positive and constructive ways of celebrating one's masculinity from another male. Men need
help in recovering and reclaiming their lives after suffering from sexual abuse. What was taken so cruelly
needs to be recovered and reclaimed in a new way —
a gentle, compassionate way. I believe that courageous
men can be instrumental in enabling other men to break
down the shadows of a false male mystique so they can
be strong and tender, resilient and compassionate, loving and respectful of himself and others. It is time to
end the darkness and to come out of the shadows and
to dismantle Thoreau's words: "The mass of men live
lives of quiet desperation."

Ministers need to be sensitive to the volatile and ex-
plosive issues that male survivors will bring with them
into the healing process. Many topics that male survivors need to talk about (male identity, reactions to
being abused by self/others, gender identity, and co-
dependency) have all been shrouded in secrecy. Men
just don't talk about such things. I believe as male
survivors get in touch with the gifts of tenderness, gentleness, and deep sensitivity in their lives, they will
begin to heal and affirm the courageous young boy that
survived and now seeks to reunite the lost child with
the adult man.

At a workshop recently, an adult male survivor
shared his painful story of abuse by a trusted clergy
person. He also shared that he was a Viet Nam vet-
eran. I thought to myself through my tears, "My God,
this man also endured the battlefield of war with his
anxiety, fear and disillusionment of authority figures.
What scars some men endure." I thank my God they
have at last found a safe place to unburden their stories,

their inner pain and all they had to do to camouflage such terrible abuse. Today in a safe room with other men and women survivors this man shared his painful childhood secret and was able to be vulnerable and at the same time deeply respected and understood.

One man came to a retreat for survivors with his teddy bear. He shared that this little bear reminded him of his inner child, a lost little boy who needed healthy and appropriate nurturing. Today, this male survivor takes good care of the little boy within. This man is valiant. He is now a loving father of two children.

No longer do we need to have masks that hide our tears and fears. It is so important for all survivors, and especially for men, to work through their anger at a trusted authority figure who abused them and also abused their authority. This is a terrible misuse of power. Let us join together with valiant men and valiant women as they dare to survive and believe in a tomorrow of sunshine and peace.

Remember Your Heritage

Little one so filled with tears
How beautiful you are!
Born in time
You are so much more
Than the child whom most see.
Remember your heritage.
Bruised and battered and broken
Are not the parents of your spirit.
Earth bore you from her gentle womb
Air fathered you in sustaining love
E'er before you knew betrayal

By the surrogates who raised you.
Remember your noble birth.
A Higher Power than any flesh and blood
Could conceive
Forms the center of your being
Cradling your inner child with love
And tenderness.
Remember your divine spark.
The sun who enlightens your day
Is the brother within you named Courage.
Who brings to light
The dark secrets of abusers.
Water who cleanses and purifies
Is your sister within named Healing
Who brings peace and refreshment
To your troubled soul.
Remember your family line.
Incest is not my father.
Nor abuse my mother at all.
They were a heritage of people
Not big enough or little enough
To be my parents.
I remember my heritage:
It is of nature.
I remember my lineage:
It is most human.
I celebrate my origin:
I am of God.

—from *Men Surviving Incest*

Chapter 14

Pilgrims of Grace

ભ્

"As you have heard from the beginning, his command is that you walk in love."
— 2 John 6

A SURVIVOR'S JOURNEY will probably be a life-long journey each day revealing a little bit more of joy and a little bit less of pain. It is a journey that will enable persons who have been sexually abused to release their secret, unbearable anxieties and troubled spirits. It is a journey that pastoral care workers, professionals, support persons and other courageous healers will embrace because they care. They care deeply that another human being who has suffered violations of the body and the spirit will feel and experience the grace of friendship, therapy, spiritual encouragement and consolation so that they can step forward out of the shadows and live life more peacefully and with great, well-deserved dignity. This healing, as I have expressed throughout this book, is a very arduous journey. It has many heartaches, setbacks, and losses that no human being should ever have had to endure. It is also a journey of tremendous faithfulness and courage.

Survivors who step forward to help others who have been abused become "Pilgrims of Grace," immersing themselves in the journey of healing life's deepest wounds, discovering new paths, creating new roots, making new friends and finding new ways to celebrate life. These "Pilgrims of Grace" dare to share their gifts of understanding, respecting and loving others with great dignity and empathy. These "Pilgrims of Grace" know the courage it takes to want to "keep on" when everything seems so lost, so very unbearable. It is truly a gift of grace to lift up one's own deeply wounded spirit and bind up one's own brokenness so that another survivor can see some light in the darkness. To behold the face of Jesus in another companion is truly a gift and a blessing for great healing and everlasting thanksgiving.

It has been and will continue to be a journey of ups and downs. Perhaps our graced journey will touch someone else's dark shadow and give them the courage to say: "I was abused," or "I am being abused," or "I am abusing someone, please help me." We will never know where our grace to be courageous and faithful will be heard and responded to by an aching spirit or a despondent heart that longs to be set free. The real gift is that others might pick up this book and feel that my words are their words or the words of someone they are very concerned about. Survivors need to know and be told that they have the ability, capacity and courage to reach out to someone for assistance in their healing journey. As "Pilgrims of Grace," we can enable each other to channel our pain, depression or addictions into meaningful, healing activities of work, play and prayer.

None of this will be easy. A journey to recover from sexual abuse will not be neat, orderly or peacefilled. At times we will feel we are plodding through the mud and filth of yet another memory, flashback or panic attack and leaving a cloud on what was to be a peace-filled day or activity. But survivors don't give up. I've said it a million times to myself. I only hope and pray that by surviving such indignities, we can truly believe that we are good, holy and brave people who deserve to be healed and to feel safe, protected and worthwhile. If you are overwhelmed and feeling very low or depressed today, believe that tomorrow you can start over and step forward into the sunlight because you have amazing grace to heal the deep wounds caused by sexual abuse.

Ministers of healing can recognize this quality in a survivor's life as the grace of the pilgrim dancer daring to dance with joy and leap with courage into life. Together we can bring the comfort of a loving creator and the blessing of a redeeming Lord to the hearts and souls of those who have been abused and help them discover the gift of new life. That is what a pilgrim does — especially a "Pilgrim of Grace." They learn to treasure the moment, the space and even the darkness and to come forward with a renewed belief in one's capacity to survive and to celebrate the journey.

> *"Grace has brought you safe thus far,*
> *And grace will lead you home."*
> — Amazing Grace

As we walk together in this journey of healing, we will learn to let our barriers down and not let our fears gobble us up. We will be set free to see a threshold of roses waiting to surround us and to proclaim that nothing is too good to be true. Your life, though scarred, is not damaged forever. You can have a beautiful, holy and happy life if you trust yourself to say: "I am Valiant. I am Brave. I am Steadfast. I am Courageous. I am a Healer. I survived, but more than that, I am a person reclaiming life in grace-filled and faith-filled ways. This is my journey and perhaps it is part of your journey or someone you care about ever so deeply."

We can be faithful and true when we walk together, believe and hope that life is a gift a survivor deserves to celebrate. We need to believe that tomorrows do come and they will continue to have moments of resurrection, celebration and challenge. But most important for all of us is to remember that a loving God is everywhere and he never leaves us. God's love is truly everlasting.

> *"I thank God for my handicaps,*
> *for through them,*
> *I have found myself,*
> *my work,*
> *and my God."*
>
> —Helen Keller

The journey to survive is not over. I have a tomorrow to embrace, to live and to celebrate.

Epilogue

ॐ

T HIS EPILOGUE does not attempt to fill in the gaps of my book or add one last word I think needs to be said so that the reader will understand what abuse is and how terrible its effects are on an individual and society. But rather, it is my opportunity to say to all survivors and to those who minister to us, do not fear to hope.

> *"Hope is for pilgrim people*
> *searching for a promised land;*
> *Hope is like a rose in winter*
> *or an open hand.*
> *It celebrates the light of morning,*
> *While working in the dark and cold*
> *It gathers us together*
> *to share what we've been told*
> *Do not fear to Hope."*
>
> — refrain from song *Do Not Fear to Hope*
> by Rory Cooney

It is my hope that in some small way by sharing my pain and my struggle to keep on surviving that I have brought some *light* into your hearts and spirits so you may understand the call we all have to live with reverence and dignity; to share kindness and respect with all people; to dare to walk courageously into the great darkness called abuse and be healing lights of compassion, comfort and justice.

My survival, and the survival of so many men, women and children who have or are being sexually abused is our inner strength. It is also a reminder to our society and church ministers that there is much more for all of us to do for:

- our children — all the children in our world

- battered men and women

- those suffering from mental illness

- the homeless persons wandering our streets

- the ending of wars

- the ending of domestic violence

- persons suffering with AIDS

- the healing of addictions

- better ways of dealing with conflict

The list could go on and on. It is my continued hope that survivors need no longer suffer in silence but can feel the healing power of love calling forth their gifts of courage, steadfast faith and enduring love. When a person dares to walk into the wilderness of another's life and feel the pain, discomfort and fears and does not walk away, but rather, lifts up the spirit and enables a survivor to rejoice in community — this is a holy opportunity. It is my hope that this book will be a light in the darkness and enable each reader to recognize that in some small way we can be courageous healers for one another.

The church is not just a building. It is a heart, a place where we, as a community of believers, can gather and celebrate our journeys that have in some mysterious way led us to the cross to receive the blessing and to be the heart, the hands, the feet, the healing touch of gentle compassion for a wounded, broken abused heart that so much yearns to be whole, holy and loving.

May we have the courage to speak the truth with dignity and to create a world where love never fails.

> *Love bears all things.*
> *Believes all things.*
> *Hopes all things.*
> *Endures all things.*
> *Love . . . never fails.*

This is the last page of the book . . . perhaps it is the holiest page of this book . . . it is with this page that I end this book but not my journey to be a sign of joy and hope in darkness and injustice. It is on this page that I am reminded of the terrible inhuman violations that happen every day in war torn countries. It is on this page that I am reminded of four American women who went to El Salvador to bring peace and solace to the hearts of many living in great fear. It is on this page that I recall that five more American women gave their lives in Liberia while ministering to the poor and the frightened. It is on this page that I ponder the unknown names of the thousands of women and children in Yugoslavia whose lives have been shattered by rape and inhuman sexual assaults.

We can no longer bear this pain in silence, disbelief or indifference. We are responsible for one another . . . may we have the courage and faithfulness to walk with the very wounded and find Christ glorified.

> *"Many of those who sleep in the dust*
> *of the earth shall awake . . .*
> *And those who lead the many*
> *to justice shall be*
> *like the stars forever."*
> —Mass of All Souls Day

Renascence ... Rebirth

The barren branches
   of a wintry tree
Despoiled and bleak
   For all to see
Yet hoping still
   It yet may be

We, too, despoiled
   Abused, disgraced
   Yet hoping too
We yet may be

Take courage, then,
   A victor be
For life once flowed
   Upon a tree.

       — Ann Kinsella, OP

Appendix

 C❧

W HEN A MINISTER sits down with a survivor of
abuse, it can truly be a healing moment, a moment of shared grace. It would be very beneficial for the
minister to share this feeling with a survivor by saying
something like:

*Today is a grace-filled journey . . . to discover grace, to
celebrate grace, and to be a gift of grace for one another.*

I also suggest a healing definition of grace — as a
gift, a precious treasure, an ennobling and comforting
source of goodness and kindness that we are called
forth to share with one another, especially during times
of trial, illness and despair. This type of welcome is holy
and comforting to someone who very often comes with
a spirit that is devastated and deeply wounded.

After or midway through a session, a minister might
ask the survivor if he/she would like to share some
prayers of grace during this sad, lonely and fearful time.
(Some survivors who suffer from PTSD need to have
gentle moments of prayer. This enables them to feel
calm, peacefilled and comforted).

Allow time for the survivor to name some moments
and people of grace that have enabled them to have

hope, to believe in themself and to find a God of peace, compassion and hope.

Grace is . . .

A wellspring of peace . . . . Be our guide.
A model of strength   Be our guide.
A model of gentleness   Be our guide.
A model of trust   Be our guide.
A model of courage   Be our guide.
A model of patience   Be our guide.
A model of risk   Be our guide.
A model of openness   Be our guide.

Grace is . . .

A gift of liberation   Pray for us.
A gift of letting go   Pray for us.
A gift of nonviolence   Pray for us.
A gift of suffering   Pray for us.
A gift of contradiction   Pray for us.
A gift of resurrection   Pray for us.

Grace is . . .

Each person says _____ (*name*) _____ is a gift of Grace.

Litany of Grieving

A minister can offer a prayer to lift up the spirit of a survivor who is dealing with the many losses that abuse has caused in his/her life.

Opening Prayer

Don't be afraid, I'm holding you close in the
   darkness
My love and my grace will carry you through the
   long night
Though you be burdened, I will cradle you deep
   in my heart
Though you be weary, my wings will enfold you
   with rest... one day at a time. Amen.

—Colleen Fulmer

A Psalm for Survivors Rising

Leader: Here and there, men and women are rising,
         everywhere men and women are rising,
         rising from the darkness.

All: Here and there, I am rising,
         everywhere, I am rising
         rising from the darkness.

Left Side:	*Right Side:*
From our silence	We are rising
From our bondage	We are rising
From exclusion	We are rising
From exploitation	We are rising
From rape and incest	We are rising
From sexual assaults	We are rising
From terrible guilt	We are rising
From all afflictions	We are rising
From addictions	We are rising
Against all obstacles	We are rising

Leader: Here and there men and women are rising,
everywhere, men and women are
rising, rising from the darkness.

Left Side: Into hope   *Right Side:* We are rising
Into freedom   We are rising
Into partnership   We are rising
Into significance   We are rising
Into the future   We are rising

Leader: Here and there, men and women are rising,
everywhere, men and women are rising,
rising from the darkness.

Closing Prayer

Leader: You who hear your children's cries
You whose own child was abused,
    speak from your warm, compassionate
      heart.
And say to your wounded sons and
      daughters,
    you were a victim,
      you did nothing wrong.
        Do not let guilt consume you.
Yes, speak from your warm, compassionate
      heart,
and say to your wounded sons and
      daughters:
Peace . . . of the new fallen snow be with you.
Peace . . . of the forest path be with you.

Peace ... of the singing birds be with you.
Peace ... of the companions walking gently
beside you.
Peace ... forever and ever. Amen.

Themes and Scripture
to Reflect on with Survivors

Anguish: For Thou art my lamp, O Lord;
                       and
              The Lord will lighten my darkness.

— 2 Samuel 22:29

Depression: The wilderness and the solitary place
              shall be glad for them;
                       and
              The desert shall rejoice, and blossom as
              the rose.

— Isaiah 35:1

Faith: I am the way, the truth and the life.

— John 14:6

Hope: For the Lord thy God bringeth thee into
              a good land, a land of brooks of water,
              of fountains, and depths that spring out
              of valleys and hills.

— Deuteronomy 8:7

Journey: Thou has set all the borders of the earth;
              thou hast made summer and winter.

— Psalm 74:17

Joy: Let the field be joyful, and all that is therein; then shall all the trees of the wood rejoice before the Lord.

— Psalm 96:12

Sorrow/Loss: Many waters cannot quench love; neither can the floods drown it.

— Song of Solomon 8:7

Glossary

CR

Abuse. To use wrongly, misuse, mistreat; violent words, actions or deeds that scar forever.

Multiple Personality Disorder (MPD) — Dissociative Disorder. (a) The existence within the person of two or more distinct personalities or personality states (each with its own relatively enduring pattern of perceiving, relating to, and thinking about the environment and self. **(b)** At least two of these personalities or personality states take full control of the person's behavior (Colin A. Ross, M.D. *Multiple Personality Disorder,* NY: John Wiley & Sons, 1989).

Post Traumatic Stress Disorder (PTSD). PTSD was first named by the American Psychiatric Association (DSM-III, 1980). The condition is a physiological, emotional, psychological, and behavioral disorder, caused by traumatic events outside the range of usual human experience: threats to life or physical integrity, serious threats or harm committed against one's children, spouse, or other close relatives or friends, sudden destruction of property, home, or community, and witnessing serious injury or death from an accident or act of violence. All may violate the survivor's personal safety, integrity, and radically alter his or her sense of internal equilibrium and identity.

Pro Survivor. A person who affirms a survivor's journey and who befriends the survivor in some helpful and supportive manner that enables healing to take place.

Trauma. An injury violently produced; such as emotional shock having lasting psychic effects. The trauma usually affects every facet of a person's life.

Bibliography

⋘

Nonfiction

Ackerman, Robert, Ph.D., and Dee Graham. *Too Old to Cry: Abused Teens in Today's America.* Blue Ridge Summit, PA: Tab Books, 1990.

Amber. *Daddy, Please Say You're Sorry.* Minneapolis: Comp-Care Publishers, 1992.

Angelou, Maya. *I Know Why the Caged Bird Sings.* New York: Bantam Books, 1980.

Bass, Ellen and Laura Davis. *The Courage to Heal.* New York: Harper & Row Publishers, 1992, 2nd edition.

Black, Claudia, Ph.D. *Double Duty.* New York: Ballantine Books, 1990.

Black, Claudia, Ph.D. *It's Never Too Late to Have a Happy Childhood.* New York: Ballantine Books, 1989.

Bly, Robert. *Iron John: A Book About Men.* Reading, MA: Addison-Wesley, 1990.

Burgess, Ann, and Carol Hartman. *Sexual Exploitation in Professional Relationships.* Washington, DC: APA Press, 1989.

Capacchione, Ph.D., Lucia. *Recovery of Your Inner Child.* New York: Simon & Schuster, 1991.

Cassidy, Sheila. *Sharing the Darkness: The Spirituality of Caring.* Maryknoll, NY: Orbis Books, 1991.

Chester, Pellauer, and Beyajian. *Sexual Assault and Abuse: A Handbook for Clergy and Religious Professionals.* San Francisco: Harper & Row, 1987.

Clark, Sister Ave, O.P. *Roses: Healing Booklet of Prayers for Adult Survivors of Abuse.* Sisters of St. Dominic (555 Albany Avenue, Amityville, NY 11701), 1990.

117

Clark, Sister Ave, O.P. *Recovering From Childhood Sexual Abuse.* Saint Meinrad, IN: CareNote: Abbey Press, 1991.

Cohen, Barry. *Multiple Personality From the Inside Out.* ed. Esther Giller and Lynn W. Baltimore, MD: Sidran Press, 1991.

Curtois, Christine. *Healing the Incest Wound.* New York: W. W. Norton, Inc. 1988.

Davis, Laura. *Allies in Healing.* New York: Harper Collins Publishers, 1991.

Dean, Amy E. *Night Light: A Book of Nighttime Meditations.* Center City, MN: Hazelden Books, 1986.

DeSalvo, Louise. *Virginia Woolf: Impact of Childhood Sexual Abuse on Her Life and Work.* New York: Ballantine Books, 1989.

Evert, Kathy, and Inie Bijkok. *When You're Ready: A Woman's Healing from Childhood Physical and Sexual Abuse by Her Mother.* Walnut Creek, CA: Launch Press, 1987.

Fortune, Marie. *Keeping the Faith: Questions and Answers for the Abused Woman.* San Francisco: Harper & Row, 1987.

Fortune, Marie. *Is Nothing Sacred?* San Francisco: Harper & Row, 1989.

Gannon, Patrick, Ph.D. *Soul Survivors: A New Beginning for Adults Abused As Children.* Englewood Cliffs, NJ: Prentice-Hall, 1989.

Gateley, Edwina. *I Hear a Seed Growing.* Trabuco Canyon, CA: Source Books, 1992.

Geyer, Melanie C. *Human Boundaries and Personal Abuse.* Denville, NJ: Dimension Books, 1992.

Gil, Eliana, Ph.D. *United We Stand.* Walnut Creek, CA: Launch Press, 1990.

Grubman-Black, Stephen D. *Broken Boys/Mending Men: Recovering From Childhood Sexual Abuse.* Blue Ridge Summit, PA: TAB Books, 1990.

Herman, Judith Lewis, M.D. *Father-Daughter Incest.* Cambridge, MA: Harvard University Press, 1981.

Herman, Judith Lewis, M.D. *Trauma and Recovery.* New York: Harper Collins Publishers, 1992.

Hunter, H. *Abused Boys: Neglected Victims of Sexual Abuse.* Lexington, MA: D. C. Heath Co., 1990.

Hutson, Joan. *My Heart's Journal.* Notre Dame, IN: Ave Maria Press, 1991.

Imbers, Annie, and Inehe Jonker. *Christianity and Incest.* Minneapolis: Fortress Press, 1992

Ingersori, S. and S. Patton. *Treating Perpetrators of Sexual Abuse.* Lexington, MA: D. C. Heath Co., 1990.

In God's Care (Daily Meditations on Spirituality in Recovery). Center City, MN: Hazelden Books, 1990.

Kane, Evangeline. *Recovering from Incest: Imagination and the Healing Process.* Boston, MA: Sigo Press, 1989.

Leehan, James. *Pastoral Care for Survivors of Family Abuse.* Louisville: Westminster/John Knox Press, 1989.

Lew, Mike, M.Ed. *Victims No Longer: Men Recovering from Incest and Other Sexual Child Abuse.* New York: Harper & Row, 1990.

Lukas, Christopher and Henry M. Seiden, Ph.D. *Silent Grief: Living in the Wake of Suicide.* New York: Scribner's & Sons, 1988.

Maine, Margo, Ph.D. *Father Hunger.* Carlsbad, CA: Gurze Books, 1991.

Maltz, Wendy. *The Sexual Healing Journey: A Guide for Survivors of Sexual Abuse.* New York: Harper Collins Publishers, 1991.

Martin, Del. *Battered Wives.* San Francisco: Volcano Press, 1981.

Miller, Alice. *Thou Shalt Not Be Aware.* New York: Meridian Books, 1986.

Morneau, Bishop Robert F. *Mantras from a Poet: Jessica Powers.* Kansas City, MO: Sheed & Ward Publishers, 1991.

Nestingen, Signe L. and Laurel Ruth Lewis. *Growing Beyond Abuse Workbook for Survivors of Sexual Exploitation and Childhood Sexual Abuse.* Minneapolis: Omni Recovery, 1990.

Nemeck, Francis, OMI and Miriam Therese Coombs. *O Blessed Night.* New York: Alba House, 1991.

O'Leary, Daniel. *Windows of Wonder.* Mahwah, NJ: Paulist Press, 1992.

Perrin, Thomas. *I Am an Adult Who Grew up in an Alcoholic Family.* Skillman, NJ: Perrin/Treggett Booksellers, 1990.

Robinson, Rita. *Survivors of Suicide.* Santa Monica, CA: IBS Press, 1989.

Ross, Colin A., M.D. *Multiple Personality Disorder: Diagnosis, Clinical Features and Treatment.* New York: John Wiley and Sons, 1989.

Rossetti, Stephen. *Slayer of the Soul: Child Sexual Abuse and the Catholic Church.* Mystic, CT: Twenty-Third Publications, 1991.

Sammon, Sean, FMS. *Alcoholism's Children: ACOA's in Priesthood and Religious Life.* New York: Alba House, 1989.

Shengold, Leonard, M.D. *Soul Murderers: The Effects of Childhood Sexual Abuse and Deprivation.* New Haven: Yale University Press, 1989.

Terr, L. *Too Scared to Cry: Psychic Trauma in Childhood.* New York: Harper & Row, 1990.

Thomas T. *Men Surviving Incest.* Notre Dame, IN: Ave Maria Press, 1992.

Wicks, Robert. *Reflections: Psychological and Spiritual Images of the Heart.* Mahwah, NJ: Paulist Press, 1990.

Wicks, Robert. *Touching the Holy.* Notre Dame, IN: Ave Maria Press, 1992.

Wood, Wendy, and Leslie Hatton. *Triumph Over Darkness.* Hillsboro, OR: Beyond Words Publishers, Inc., 1988.

Yancy, Philip. *Where Is God When It Hurts?* Grand Rapids, MI: Zondervan Publishing Co., 1990.

Fiction

Chase, Truddi. *When Rabbit Howls.* New York: E. P. Dutton Publishers, 1987.

Miller, Alice. *Possessing the Secret of Joy.* New York: Harcourt Brace Jovanovich Publishers, 1992.

Miller, Alice. *The Color Purple.* New York: Pocket Books, 1982.

Palwick, Susan. *Flying in Place: A Novel about Child Abuse.* New York: Tom Doherty Associates Book, 1992.

Spiritual

(Can be adapted for use in spiritual direction/counseling and retreat days for survivors of abuse).

Aurelio, John. *The Garden of Life: (A Story of Hope for All Ages)*. New York: Crossroad, 1989.

Berg, Richard F., C.S.C and Christine McCartney. *Depression and the Integrated Life: (A Christian Understanding of Sadness and Inner Suffering)*. New York: Alba House, 1981.

Dunn, Amy. *Once Upon a Time: (Stories of Hope from Adult Children Who Are Reclaiming Life with Great Courage)*. New York: Harper & Row, 1988.

Durka, Gloria. *Praying with Julian of Norwich*. Winona, MN: St. Mary's Press, 1989.

Fahy, Mary. *The Tree that Survived the Winter*. Mahwah, NJ: Paulist Press, 1989.

Helldorfer, Martin, D.Min. *A Guide: Prayer When Troubled*. Worcester, MA: Mercantile Printing Co., 1985.

May, Gerald G., M.D. *Addiction and Grace*. San Francisco: Harper, 1988.

O'Leary, Daniel. *Windows of Wonder: (A Spirituality of Self-Esteem)*. Mahwah, NJ: Paulist Press, 1991.

Peers, Allison. *Dark Night of the Soul*. New York: Doubleday, 1990.

Wicks, Robert J., et al. ed. *Clinical Handbook of Pastoral Counseling*. Mahwah, NJ: Paulist Press, 1985.

Wicks, Robert J. *Reflections: Psychological and Spiritual Images of the Heart*. Mahwah, NJ: Paulist Press, 1990.

Winter, Miriam Therese. *Woman Prayer . . . Woman Song: (Resources for Ritual)*. New York: Crossroad, 1990.

Winter, Miriam Therese. *Woman Witness (Part 1 and 2)*. New York: Crossroad, 1992.

A Winter's Song: A Liturgy for Women Seeking Healing from Sexual Abuse in Childhood. New York: The Pilgrim Press, 1991.

Articles

Clark, Sister Ave, O.P. "Helping the Sexually Abused." *Human Development* (Winter, 1992).

Clark, Sister Ave, O.P. "Surviving Sexual Abuse." *Human Development* (Summer,1990).

Clark, Sister Ave, O.P. "The Church's Response to Deep Wounds: Incest, Rape and Sexual Assault." *Sisters Today* (November, 1991).

Clark, Sister Ave, O.P. "Together in God We Are Whole." *Our Sunday Visitor* (1991), p. 20.

Fitzgerald, Rev. David, C.P. "Survivors of Sexual Abuse." *Human Development* (Summer, 1991).

Fortune, Marie, and Judith Hertz. A commentary on "Religious Issues in Family Violence." Center for the Prevention of Sexual and Domestic Violence (1991).

Videos

Center for Prevention of Abuse/Domestic Violence, 1914 N. 34th Street, Suite 305, Seattle, WA 98103. *Hear Their Cries: Religious Response to Child Abuse.*

Gediman, Dan. *Silent Shame: Male Survivors of Child Sexual Abuse.* Milestone Productions, P.O. Box 4962, Louisville, KY 40204.

Franciscan Communications, 1229 S. Santee Street, Los Angeles, CA 90015. *Heart to Heart Series.* For use with teachers, parents, children and adult survivors to reflect on the lost parts of their childhood. Includes sexual abuse, physical abuse, alcoholism, drugs, death/separation, divorce, looking and feeling different. A book goes with each video and with the sexual abuse book/video there is also a tape of music and script.

Krause House, P.O. Box 880, Oregon City, OR 97045. *Child Abuse Prevention.*

O.D.N. Productions, 74 Varick Street, New York, NY 10013. *No More Secrets.*

Sisters of St. Dominic, 555 Albany Avenue, Amityville, NY 11701. *A Blessing Place: Called Compassion.* A healing video for adult survivors and healers of abuse/ACOA.

The University of Wisconsin-Madison, 314 Lowell Hall, 610 Langdon Street, Madison, WI 53703. *Sexual Ethics in Ministry.*

Videos with Tapes

Bass, Ellen and Laura Davis. *The Courage to Heal: A Guide for Women Survivors of Child Sexual Abuse.* Cademon, 1995 Broadway, New York, NY 10023.

Black, Claudia, Ph.D. *Double Duty: Physical Abuse/Sexual Abuse.* Mac Publishing Co., 5005 E. 39th Avenue, Denver, CO 80207.

Clark, Sister Ave, O.P. *The Church's Response to Deep Wounds.* (NCEA Convention 1990) available from Chesapeake Audio/Video Communications, Inc., 6330 Howard Lane, Elkridge, MD 21227.

Clark, Sister Ave., O.P. *The Compassionate School: Hope for the Future.* (NCEA Convention, 1992) available from Chesapeake Audio/Video Communications, Inc., 6330 Howard Lane, Elkridge, MD 21227.

Davis, Laura. *Allies in Healing: When the Person You Love Was Sexually Abused As a Child.* Harper Audio, 10 East 53rd Street, New York, NY 10022.

Halpern, Steven. *Recovering from Co-dependency.* Sound RX, P.O. Box 1439, San Rafael, CA 94915.

Sheehan, Barbara, S.P. *Caring for God's People: Meeting Critical Pastoral Needs.* (Includes tapes on bereavement, chronically mentally ill, dysfunctional families, incest survivors, elderly and a tape to become an effective caregiver). St. Anthony Messenger Press, 1615 Republic Street, Cincinnati, OH 45210.

Sweeney, Richard J. *You and Your Shadow: Discovering and Accepting Your Hidden Self.* St. Anthony Messenger Press, 1615 Republic Street, Cincinnati, OH 45210.

Newsletters

American Association of Suicidology
2459 South Ash
Denver, CO 80222

Associates in Education and Prevention in Pastoral Practice
27 Pojac Point
N. Kingstown, RI 02852
401-884-3741
(Main purpose is to prevent sexual/domestic violence in communities of faith).

CareNotes
Abbey Press
One Caring Place
St. Meinrad, IN 47577

Center for the Prevention of Sexual/Domestic Violence
1914 North 34th Street
Suite 105
Seattle, WA 98103
206-634-1903

Friends for Survival, Inc. (Suicide Survivors)
5701 Lerner Way
Sacramento, CA 95823

Lifeline Institute Organization of SOS (Survivors of Suicide)
9108 Lakewood Drive, S.W.
Tacoma, WA 98499
1-800-422-2552

NCPCA Memorandum
National Committee for Prevention of Child Abuse
332 S. Michigan Avenue
Chicago, IL 60604
(312) 663-3520

Many Voices (Dissociative Disorders)
P.O. Box 2639
Cincinnati, OH 45201-2639

Project Benjamin Archdiocese of Milwaukee
3501 South Lake Drive
P.O. Box 07912
Milwaukee, WI 53207-0912
(Pastoral response to persons involved in sexual abuse especially if the abuse has occurred within the context of the Church)

Seeds of Hope
3100 Midwest Road
Oak Brook, IL 60521

Stauros Newsletter (Reflections on Human Suffering)
Catholic Theological Union
5401 S. Cornell Avenue
Chicago, IL 60615-5698

Survivorship (Ritualistic Abuse)
3181 Mission #139
San Francisco, CA 94110

The Cutting Edge
P.O. Box 20819
Cleveland, OH 44120

The VELVETEEN Newsletter (for incest survivors)
I.S. P.O. Box 2040
Hillside Manor Branch
New Hyde Park, NY 11040

Trauma Recovery Publications
P.O. Box 6689
Columbus, GA 31907
(12 Step Spirituality for survivors of violence/post traumatic stress disorder)

Voices (Victims of Incest Can Emerge Survivors)
P.O. Box 148309
Chicago, IL 60614

"When I Call for Help"
U.S. Catholic Conference
Washington, DC 20017-1194
A Pastoral Response to Domestic Violence Against Women

Referrals

ACOA (Adult Children of Alcoholics)
200 Park Avenue
31st Floor
New York, NY 10166

Alcoholics Anonymous
468 Park Avenue South
New York, NY 10016

American Anorexia/Bulimia Associates
133 Cedar Lane
Teaneck, NJ 07666

Center for Abuse Recovery and Empowerment
The Psychiatric Institute of Washington, D.C.
4228 Wisconsin Avenue N.W.
Washington, D.C. 20016

Cornell Medical Center
New York, NY

Ecclesial Center (for religious/clergy)
Girard, PA

Genesis House
922 West Addison
Chicago, IL 60613
(A house of hospitality and nurturance for women in prostitution)

Golden Valley Health Center
4101 Golden Valley Road
Golden Valley, MN 55422

IMPACT
323 South Pearl Street
Denver, CO 80209
(For those abused in counseling and therapy)

Incest Resources
46 Pleasant Street
Cambridge, MA 02139
(Includes information on deaf persons being abused)

Institute of the Pennsylvania Hospital
111 N. 49th Street
Philadelphia, PA 19139

LINKUP
P.O. Box 1268
Wheeling, IL 60090
(For victims of clergy sexual abuse, formerly called VOCAL)

Mary's Pence
P.O. Box 29078
Chicago, IL 60629-9078
(funds ministries to/for oppressed women)

McLean Hospital
115 Mill Street
Belmont, MA 02178

Menninger Clinic
5800 S.W. 6th Street
Topeka, KS 66601

MP/Dignity
P.O. Box 4367
Boulder, CO 80306-4367

National Center for Prosecution of Child Abuse
American Prosecutors
Research Institute
1033 North Fairfax Street
Suite 200
Alexandria, VA 22314

National Child Abuse Hotline
1-800-422-4453

Overeaters Anonymous National Office
4025 Spencer Street
Suite 203
Torrance, CA 90503

Phobia Society of America
P.O. Box 42514
Washington, D.C. 20015

P.L.E.A.
356 West Zia Road
Santa Fe, NM 87505
(National Organization for Male Survivors)

Servants of the Paraclete (for religious/clergy)
Jemez Springs, NM 87025

Silver Hill Hospital
208 Valley Road
New Canaan, CT 06840

S.N.A.P.
Survivors Network (who were abused by priests)
8025 S. Honore
Chicago, IL 60620

St. Louis Centre of Holistic Healing
121 West Monroe Avenue
Kirkwood, MO 63122

St. Luke's Institute (for religious/clergy)
Washington, D.C.

Society for PTSD (Post Traumatic Stress Disorder)
P.O. Box 1564
Lancaster, PA 17603-1564

Southdown (for religious/clergy)
Ontario, Canada

South Oaks Mental Health Center
400 Sunrise Highway
Amityville, NY 11701

The National Alliance for the Mentally Ill
Suite 302
Arlington, VA 22201
(703-524-7600)

Villa St. John Vianney Hospital (for religious/clergy)
Box 219
Woodbine Avenue/Lincoln Highway
Downingtown, PA 19335

ABOUT THE AUTHOR

Sister Ave Clark has been an Amityville Dominican for over thirty years. She has worked for over twenty years with persons with disabling conditions in the Diocese of Brooklyn. It was here among those struggling with disability, illness and acceptance that she gained courage to embrace her painful past and to break her silence as a victim of rape and sexual assaults. She credits her recovery and ongoing journey to healing to a wonderful Dominican community, a dedicated and professional therapist and to other survivors and support friends.

She wrote this book to reclaim her inner goodness and to reach out to other survivors and say, "I understand. Let us walk gently together into the light called love and compassion." Today, she offers retreats and days of prayer for survivors of sexual abuse and ACOAs.

Another Fine Book from Resurrection Press

A PATH TO HOPE
for Parents of Aborted Children and Those
Who Minister to Them

John J. Dillon
Foreword by James P. Lisante

The pain and distress of Post-Abortion Syndrome are gradually and gradually and alarming coming to light as counselors see more and more victims of P.A.S. who cry out for healing. Drawing on his own considerable experience with parents of aborted children. Fr. Dillon succinctly describes the spiritual and psychological aftermath of abortion and offers solid guidelines and compassionate advice to those who counsel, minister to or journey with them. The issue of excommunication is discussed, and guidelines for a Healing Service are included.

"Should be a required textbook for anyone who wants to be involved in post-abortion ministry."

VICKI THORN, FOUNDER
PROJECT RACHEL

"A gift for all who seek to be healers and reconcilers . . . a special grace for the hurting seeking the freedom of God's boundless love." FR. JAMES P. LISANTE, DIRECTOR
OFFICE OF FAMILY MINISTRY
DIOCESE OF ROCKVILLE CENTRE

"John Dillon understands the pain of aborted parents and gets right to where they are hurting. This is a wonderful how-to book." SUSAN KLESZEWSKI, M.S.W., L.C.S.W.
PSYCHOTHERAPIST

Fr. John J. Dillon is a spokesperson for Project Rachel in the Diocese of Rockville Centre, NY, and has lectured extensively throughout the country on the issue of post-abortion ministry.

ISBN 1-878718-00-2   80 pp. $5.95

Other Titles Available from Resurrection Press

Our Spirit-Life Audiocassette Collection

Resurrection Press books and cassettes are available in your local religious bookstore. In case of difficulty, or if you wish to be on our mailing list for our up-to-date announcements, please write or phone:

Resurrection Press
P.O. Box 248, Williston Park, NY 11596
1-800-89 BOOKS